THE SOURCES FOR THE LIFE OF CHRIST

IS VOLUME

67

OF THE

Twentieth Century Encyclopedia of Catholicism

UNDER SECTION

VI

THE WORD OF GOD

IT IS ALSO THE

92ND

VOLUME IN ORDER OF PUBLICATION

Edited by HENRI DANIEL-ROPS of the Académie Française

THE SOURCES FOR THE LIFE OF CHRIST

By FRANÇOIS AMIOT, P.S.S.,
AMÉDÉE BRUNOT, S.C.J.,
JEAN DANIÉLOU, S.J.,
HENRI DANIEL-ROPS

Translated from the French by P. J. HEPBURNE-SCOTT

HAWTHORN BOOKS · PUBLISHERS · *New York*

First Edition, August, 1962

NIHIL OBSTAT

Joannes M. T. Barton, S.T.D., L.S.S.

 Censor Deputatus

IMPRIMATUR

E. Morrogh Bernard

 Vicarius Generalis

Westmonasterii, die XII JUNII, MCMLXII

CONTENTS

CHAPTER I

JESUS, AN HISTORICAL PERSON

by François Amiot, P.S.S.

Did Christ exist? Is it really necessary to discuss this question? Can it be seriously maintained that the greatest character in all history existed only in the imagination of deluded disciples? Such a theory was advanced, not forty years ago, by Paul Louis Couchoud, in a book which caused some stir, *Le Mystère de Jésus*. The author cheerfully invited the faithful to free themselves from the doctrine of the incarnate Son of God and to admit that the personality of Jesus was a complete forgery, an ingenious construction made up of prophetic oracles foretelling the future Messiah. Even the most radical critics, led by Loisy and Guignebert, protested at such a defiance of common sense. Fr Lagrange, the well-known biblical scholar of Jerusalem, never given to strong words, described Couchoud's theory, after careful examination, as "definitive absurdity". A brilliant apologist, Abbé Werhlé, remarked, not without malice, that Couchoud treated the argument from prophecy with a consistency unusual in liberal critics. There is no error which does not contain some truth. But with Abbé Werhlé this was only a passing reflection in the course of an energetic rejection of the negations of Couchoud, who stood revealed as an amateur exegete and moralist.

Such aberrations leave one speechless. But they can make an unfortunate impression and may seriously disturb those who have not studied Christian origins. It is, then, worth while reminding ourselves how far the existence of Christ is a firmly established truth; otherwise we should have to abandon all historical certainty.

The earthly life of Christ has left some traces in secular history. Flavius Josephus, in his *Antiquities of the Jews,* mentions the condemnation of Jesus by Pontius Pilate, the existence of the Christian sect[1] and the stoning by Herod Agrippa of James, "the brother of Jesus, called the Christ".[2] In connection with the burning of Rome, Tacitus tells in a famous passage how the emperor Nero tried to divert the people's wrath by accusing the Christians, whom he handed over to the most refined tortures. He adds: "Christus, the founder of this name, had been condemned to death by the procurator Pontius Pilate in the reign of Tiberius."[3] And he scornfully remarks that this pernicious sect, sprung from Judaea, had spread in the Empire and particularly in Rome. Another historian, Suetonius, alludes to the expulsion from Rome by Claudius of the Jews, "who had become, at the instigation of Chrestus [an obvious corruption of Christus], a permanent cause of disorder".[4] Finally, about the same period, the writer Pliny the Younger, governor of Bithynia, in a famous letter to the emperor Trajan, notes among other details about the Christians of Asia Minor, that they "were in the habit of meeting before dawn on fixed days and singing hymns to Christ as to a god".[5] These texts, though somewhat meagre for our liking, are nevertheless significant; their brevity is explained by the fact that Christianity, which sprang from Judaism, was at first not clearly distinguished from it and attracted little attention.

The situation changes visibly when we consider the Christian sources. St Paul's epistles, which are mostly anterior to the definitive record of the Gospels, and therefore of unique historical value, allude to numerous incidents in the Saviour's life. Although they do not describe them in detail (which

---

[1] *Antiq.*, XVIII, 3.   [2] *Ibid.*, XX, 9.   [3] *Annals*, XV, 44.
[4] *Life of Claudius*, XXV, 4.   [5] *Letters*, X, 96.

was not their purpose), we can draw from them a summary portrait of Christ which perfectly agrees with the facts in the Gospels. They mention the birth of Jesus in the tribe of Juda, his baptism by John, the disciples who followed him, his many miracles, his transfiguration, his poverty and surpassing sanctity, the institution of the Eucharist, the agony, the betrayal by Judas, the Passion. For the Resurrection, the list of appearances in 1 Cor. 15. 5-8 is even more complete than in the Gospels.

These pieces of information, to which must be added those in the Acts of the Apostles and the other canonical epistles, have a value as evidence, and this evidence is presented with a seriousness which gives it supreme importance. From the morrow of Pentecost, the apostles assert with significant insistence that they are authentic witnesses of the crucifixion of the "author of life", of his resurrection by the power of the Father, of his glorification (Acts 2. 32; 3. 15; 5. 32), as also of his revealing and miraculous activity during his time on earth. The brief discourse of Peter before the baptism of the centurion Cornelius makes all commentary needless:

> You have heard the story, a story which ran through the whole of Judaea, though it began in Galilee, after the baptism which John proclaimed; about Jesus of Nazareth, how God anointed him with the Holy Spirit and with power, so that he went about doing good, and curing all those who were under the devil's tyranny, with God at his side. We are witnesses of all he did in the country of the Jews, and in Jerusalem. And they killed him, hanging him on a gibbet; but on the third day God raised him up again, and granted the clear sight of him, not to the people at large, but to us, the witnesses whom God had appointed beforehand; we ate and drank in his company after his rising from the dead. And he gave us a commission to preach to the people, and to bear witness that he, and none other, has been chosen by God to judge the living and the dead. All the prophets bear him this testimony, that everyone who has faith in him is to find remission of sins through his name (Acts 10. 37–43).

This passage produces a striking impression of strength and certainty. It is the same with St Paul's enumeration of the appearances of the risen Christ (1 Cor. 15. 3–8), after which the apostle boldly declares: "If Christ has not risen, then our preaching is groundless, and your faith, too, is groundless. Worse still, we are convicted of giving false testimony about God; we bore God witness that he had raised Christ up from the dead, and he has not raised him up, if it is true that the dead do not rise again. If the dead, I say, do not rise, then Christ has not risen either; and if Christ has not risen, all your faith is a delusion; you are back in your sins" (1 Cor. 15. 14–17). He could not have committed himself more explicitly, and clearly he feared no contradiction.

Between the ascension and Pentecost, when a successor to Judas in the apostolic college had to be appointed, Peter laid down as a necessary qualification that the man chosen should have been a disciple of Jesus from his baptism by John till his ascension, so as to be a competent witness of his resurrection (Acts 1. 21–2). It is precisely this period which is covered by the testimony of the Gospels.

When we approach these marvellous little books, we must remember that their human authors are, first, two eye-witnesses, the apostles Matthew and John (the possibility that their accounts were given final form by their disciples detracts nothing from the value of their evidence) and secondly, two disciples of apostles; Mark, who reports with remarkable vividness the teaching in Rome of Peter, the foremost witness of all, and Luke, who reproduces the teaching of St Paul. St Paul was always concerned about his agreement with the other apostles (Gal. 2. 2; 1 Cor. 15. 9–11), and commended to his disciple Timothy an inviolable loyalty to the deposit of faith received from them (1 Tim. 6. 20; 2 Tim. 1. 14). Matthew, Mark and Luke wrote between A.D. 60 and 63, or at latest about 70, therefore at most forty years after the events, about which they use fragmentary narratives which are much older and often quite close in time to the facts.

St John's Gospel dates from the end of the first century, but he preached long before he wrote, and at a very early date, so that some have claimed to trace his influence in Luke. Thus these four testimonies are exceptionally well qualified to give reliable information. St Luke, moreover, makes clear that he has informed himself about everything from the beginning and has planned to give an orderly narrative, so that the illustrious Theophilus, to whom he dedicates his book, may understand the certainty of the instruction he has received (Luke 1. 3–4). Again, if the facts recorded were not true, the apostolic preaching would be without foundation. St John says so in the conclusion of his Gospel: he has recorded the life and miracles of the Saviour in order to lead men to faith in his divine sonship and, by faith, to the life of which he is the source (John 20. 31). The evangelists therefore appear as witnesses particularly well placed to know what they are talking about, and their sincerity, too, is obvious; they express themselves in a tone of undefinable frankness, with a discretion which does not directly urge the reader to share their faith, but is content to relate the facts simply, without exclamations or emphasis, convinced that the facts alone are evidence enough for anyone who will consider them as honestly as they themselves have reported them.

It will doubtless be objected that the Gospels are fragmentary documents, from which it would be impossible to construct a complete biography of Christ in the modern manner. But this is something admitted by all, and is explained by the fact that the evangelists are reproducing an oral teaching which naturally had to choose from among the events, which grouped them freely for educational purposes, which was often content with an approximation in chronology and small details, and adapted the *form* of our Lord's teachings to the needs of the Churches, while always remaining scrupulously faithful to their *spirit*. In spite of certain obvious gaps, the Gospels, from their respective points of view, provide a portrait of our Saviour which is infinitively attractive,

supported by a mass of details revealing a profound knowledge of Palestine in our Lord's time, in its geographical,
social, political and religious condition. There are hundreds
of these tiny clues which presuppose well-grounded information and actual facts.

Yes, actual facts, including the miracles and resurrection
of the Saviour. We must never forget that to become a
Christian involved a radical conversion and a thorough change
in life: by adhering to Christ one committed oneself totally
for time and for eternity. None of our forebears in the faith
made this decision without closely examining a step of such
consequence, which would quickly bring with it the prospect
of persecution and death. The existence of well-established
facts and undeniable signs kept the primitive Churches from
exaggerations and imaginative distortions such as would have
accentuated Christ's divine character, after the event. Jealous
attachment to primitive tradition, constant relations between
the different Churches, resulting in continual verification,
and finally the authority of the hierarchy, would quickly have
put a stop to any such attempts. The historical existence of
Christ, apart from which the Christian faith would have been
no more than a collection of pious dreams, is one of the most
firmly established facts of history. The anti-Christian writers
of the first centuries disputed its interpretation, never its
truth. The insane postulate of a purely mythical and historically non-existent Christ is an aberration which discredits its
authors and could never be accepted by any serious mind.
Christ was a real person, a man of flesh and blood like the
rest of us (Luke 24. 39), and the faith handed on by the
apostles, the witnesses of his life, rightly professes that he
was at the same time the only Son of God, who came down
from heaven to save the world.

CHAPTER II

THE SILENCE OF JESUS' CONTEMPORARIES

by Daniel-Rops

When we consider what a stupendous adventure it was, this coming to earth of Jesus Christ, when we think of his prestige among his own people, of that "mission" of three years, all filled with miracles, it seems impossible that such events, which were to interrupt the course of history or, rather, to inaugurate a new history, could have been unknown to men who were then alive. Palestine, after all, was a department of the Roman Empire, in constant touch with the capital. The Jews, Jesus' countrymen, were numerous in Rome, and the Romans maintained troops and all the machinery of government in the Holy Land. How could the facts of those years have remained unknown to those who wrote the chronicles of the period?

Before answering this puzzling question, it may be as well to make two preliminary remarks. Our civilization is one of rapid communication, there is a regular cult of detail. Through the press, radio and television we are used to knowing all that happens in the wide world; we are told, and often shown, the incidental and the insignificant. Was it so two thousand, or even two hundred, years ago? Before this "age of wide information", those who informed their contemporaries were practically bound to confine themselves to events which caused a great stir. Now it is not at all certain that the rise of Jesus made, at the time, the sort of stir we imagine. It is difficult to number the crowds which the evangelists show us around him: were they usually more than two or three thousand? Was the "multitude" which went before him at his glorious entry into Jerusalem on Palm Sunday more than a few hundreds? The Gospels themselves show us that at the trial and crucifixion there were few people present. Agitators trying to rouse the people, even claiming to be envoys of God, Messiahs; the type was not uncommon in that period. Perhaps if we would get a just idea of the human life of Christ and the impact it made on his contemporaries, we should try to imagine how much medieval Parisians could have known of a disturbance aroused in the depths of Brittany by a self-styled prophet, followed by a few hundred peasants.

THE OFFICIAL DOCUMENTS

Do the official records of the Roman government preserve any traces of the existence of Jesus? Two kinds of archives were preserved in Rome: the *Acta senatus*, minutes of the senatorial sessions, and the *Commentarii principis*, in which was collected all the correspondence sent to the "prince", the emperor. There is no report of any debate on Christianity in the Senate. Was a report about Christ sent to Tiberius by Pontius Pilate? Very probably, but we do not possess it. St Justin the martyr, in his *Apology*, written about 150, and addressed to the emperor Antoninus Pius and his son Marcus Aurelius, alludes to these "Acts of Pilate", but in fact he seems to refer to one of those "apocryphal gospels" which then flourished, rather than to official documents. Tacitus says that the imperial archives were secret and that no one was allowed to consult them. Fifty years later, the African apologist Tertullian considered that Justin's phrase was worth repeating and declared that the judgement and death of Christ had been reported to Tiberius by Pilate. In the fourth century, pious forgers, of whom there were many, invented this document but made the mistake of inserting the name of Claudius instead of Tiberius. Needless to say, such "evidence" is worthless.

But the silence of the official records of the empire is not absolute. We possess a text of the early second century, written in 111 or 113, which gives us very interesting information about the growth of Christianity in Asia Minor, and alludes briefly to our Lord. It is a letter of Pliny the Younger. Sent by the emperor Trajan to be governor of Bithynia, he found in this province such a large number of Christians that the temples were deserted and the sacrificial victims found no buyers. Following some denunciations, he arrested and questioned several followers of the new religion. He did not find them guilty of any specific crime; the accused only stated that they "were in the habit of meeting before dawn on fixed days and singing hymns to Christ as to a god" (*Letters*, x, 96).

Trajan's reply is well known: "They must not be sought out, but if they are denounced and convicted [of professing Christianity], they must be punished." This text, eighty years after the death of Christ, is therefore very noteworthy, because it shows that at this time the new Christian sect had already assumed considerable importance. But we cannot say that it tells us anything about Jesus himself: Pliny states the effects, but is not concerned to trace the causes. In an administrative report that would have been irrelevant.

The same attitude is found in a text about forty years later, the rescript addressed by the emperor Hadrian to Minucius Fundanus, proconsul of Asia, which confirms Pliny's testimony. Minucius' predecessor had reported abuses in various anti-Christian trials: accusations which provoked disturbances, denunciations inspired by private interests. Hadrian, a wise emperor, decides that the accusers must appear in person and if they have accused falsely they are to be punished.

ROMAN AUTHORS

Lacking official records, do we find anything more in the

historians who have recorded the events of this period? Among Roman authors of the period there were several good historians. What did they know or say about Jesus? The most important is Tacitus, universally considered the most reliable of historians, a man in whom sensibility and imagination, though lively, could never spoil a critical sense rare in his time and a great honesty in the examination of documents. Writing about 116 in his *Annals* (Bk xv, ch. 44), he thus describes the first persecution the Christians had to undergo, in A.D. 64, under Nero:

> A disgraceful rumour attributed to Nero the order to start the fire. To scotch the rumour, he substituted as culprits those men, detested for their crimes, whom the crowd called Christians, and delivered them up to the most refined tortures. Christus, the founder of this name, had been condemned to death by the procurator Pontius Pilate in the reign of Tiberius. This pernicious sect, at first checked, broke out anew, not only in Judaea, the home of this disease, but in the City itself, where all things horrible and shameful in the world collect and find a vogue.

Here too we note the effects of Christian propaganda: thirty years after the death of Christ the believers in his teaching were numerous in Rome. But as to Christ himself the historian knows only the bare essential, and that essential is contained in two lines; lines which in a sense are capital, for they explode in advance the theories of all those liberal critics who claim to see in Jesus only a myth: but they scarcely satisfy our legitimate curiosity.

At about the same time Suetonius, another Roman historian, who was very serious and very skilful at handling his sources, wrote in his Lives of the Twelve Caesars that the emperor Claudius "expelled from Rome the Jews, who had been, at the instigation of Chrestus, a permanent cause of disorder" (*Life of Claudius*, xxv, 4; cf. Acts 18. 2; "Chrestus" is obviously a corruption of Christus). Of Nero he says that this emperor "inflicted punishments on the Chris-

tians, a sect which professed a new and mischievous super-
stition".

That is all, positively all that the history written by the
Romans tells us of the greatest story of all time. There can
obviously be no question of taking seriously the "Letter of
Lentulus", in which a supposed governor of Jerusalem, wholly
unknown to history, in an alleged letter addressed to the
"Senate and people of Rome"—under the empire!—tells the
story of Jesus and describes his appearance. It is a thirteenth-
century fraud, based on other apocryphal elements. Equally
worthless is a certain "Unpublished history of the City of
Vienne" in Dauphiné, quoted in the last century by a local
writer, the elder Mermet (1828), in which we are informed
that "Tiberius proposed to the Senate that Christ should be
admitted to the rank of the gods; but when the matter had
been carefully examined they were convinced that it would
be dangerous to approve a cult based on an absolute equality
between men. Further, it seemed improper to deify a person
who had been punished with the death of a slave, with the
consent of the Roman procurator." The document is the
product of sheer fantasy.

JEWISH WRITERS

If Roman authors were so meagre in information about
Jesus, were his fellow-countrymen any better informed, or
more informative? At that time, both in Palestine and in
the Diaspora, Israel could boast of several great writers. At
Alexandria lived Philo, an exact contemporary of Christ,
who was born twenty years earlier than he, and died twenty
years later. He was a notable writer, who effected the synthesis between Jewish thought and ancient philosophy. His
fifty treatises abound in historical details, but of Jesus he
says not a word. This is a case where our earlier remark
applies: Philo was a wealthy townsman and an intellect of
the highest order. It is not unduly surprising that such a person should not pay much attention to an agitator sprung

from the humblest of the people, whose doctrine, if he had one, had no connection with philosophy.

It is more curious that Justus of Tiberias, a Galilean who was born just when Christ died, did not mention Jesus in his *Chronicle*, a now lost document which extended from Moses to Herod Agrippa. Were the facts already forgotten on the hills where the Good News had been preached, around the lake of the miraculous draught of fishes? In any case, it is known that Justus said nothing. The ninth-century Byzantine historian Photius has probably given the true reason for his silence: "A Jew by race, infected with Jewish prejudices, Justus makes no mention of the coming of Christ, of the events of his life or of his miracles." It is one of those intentional and self-revealing silences.

There are, however, other Jewish texts in existence, which go back to the same period: the Talmuds. It is a known fact that these enormous treatises, drawn up between the fourth and sixth centuries in two collections, known as that of Jerusalem and that of Babylon, reproduce the teachings of the Rabbis of Israel from at least fifty or a hundred years before Christ. There must have been Rabbis, contemporary with Jesus, who could have spoken of him. Are the Talmuds silent about him? Not entirely. In many passages they make allusions, rare and veiled but unmistakable, to his person and career. It is an undeniable testimony to the reality of the existence of Jesus and his influence. The anathemas against the Christians which were added to the *Prayer of the Eighteen Benedictions* also prove the importance of the Christian phenomenon in the eyes of the Jewish doctors. But it would be absurd to claim that any valid information about Jesus could be drawn from the Talmudic texts. Those foul calumnies, unfit to be quoted here, belong not to history but to legend. This is the opinion of the most approved Jewish historians, such as the editors of the famous *Jewish Encyclopaedia*; dividing the article on *Jesus of Nazareth* into three parts, Jesus in history, in theology and in legend, it is only in the third part that they refer to the Talmuds.

THE CASE OF FLAVIUS JOSEPHUS

Josephus must be considered separately. Born in 37 or 38 and dying in 97, he was a witness immediately after the public life of Christ. In many ways he is a considerable historian. His *Antiquities of the Jews* is, with some qualifications, infinitely valuable in supplementing the data of the Old Testament on the destiny of Israel. His *Jewish War*, published about 77, and therefore very soon after the catastrophe which finally overwhelmed the chosen people, is a priceless document. The man himself is far from attractive. A member of the priestly aristocracy whose opportunism accommodated itself to the Roman yoke, he is vain, self-satisfied and far too obsequious. He tells us many highly edifying details about himself: that at the age of thirteen he was so advanced in theology that the Jerusalem Rabbis used to call him in for consultation; that when sixteen years old, inspired by fervour, he had fled to the desert, mortifying his body with ascetic practices. In fact, he very soon went to Rome and indulged in profitable intrigues. When the supreme struggle of the Jews began in 66, he procured himself a command, but in a manner similar to that which Bazaine is suspected (perhaps unjustly) to have used at Metz in 1870. There is one story in particular, of a place hotly besieged, the defenders deciding to kill one another to avoid falling into the hands of the legionaries, and choosing Josephus by lot to be the last survivor and surrender the place, which smells very suspect. The fact remains that this Jewish general ended the war as a personal friend of his conqueror Vespasian, to whom he had predicted that he would one day be emperor. He added his master's name, Flavius, to his own, just like a freed slave, and so wallowed in flattery that he did not hesitate to write that the true Messiah expected by Israel was, undoubtedly, Vespasian.

The traits of his character must not be forgotten when we come to estimate the attitude of Josephus, surnamed Flavius. Was he totally ignorant of Jesus and Christianity? His *Antiquities* appeared in 93. It seems obvious that he knew about Christianity. By 57 it was twenty years old; the Church then held an important place in Jerusalem; when St Paul arrived in the Holy City in that year, his presence provoked a riot (Acts 21 and 26) and he was arrested. Did the future historian not take note of the episode? When Josephus was in Rome in 64, Nero's persecution was just beginning. Introduced to influential circles by his friend the Jewish actor Alityrus, did he hear nothing of the discussions about Christ which were exciting all Roman Jewry?

Two contemporaries of Jesus are mentioned by Josephus: John the Baptist, whose teaching and execution he reports perfectly accurately, and James, the first bishop of Jerusalem, whose stoning he relates and whom he describes, with a touch of contempt, as "the brother of Jesus, called the Christ". These allusions are precious, because they prove that Flavius Josephus indisputably considered Jesus to be an historical character, that he never doubted his existence.

But has he any more to tell us? In the eighteenth book of his *Antiquities* we read this amazing passage:

> About this time appeared Jesus, a wise man, *if he must be called a man.* For he did marvellous works, he was the teacher of those who receive the truth with joy, and he drew after him many Jews and also many Gentiles. *This man was the Christ.* On the accusation of the chief men of our nation, Pilate condemned him to the cross; but his believers did not give up their love for him; *for on the third day he appeared to them, risen again, as the divine prophets had foretold, just as they foretold a thousand other marvels about him.* The sect exists to this day and was given the name of Christians, after him (xviii, 3).

The italics in the above are our own. If Josephus really wrote these passages, he thereby signed his adherence to

Christianity. Now, for the last three centuries these three lines have provoked bitter discussions. Some say that they break the thread of the discourse; others retort that the style is precisely that of Josephus. They invoke Eusebius who, at the beginning of the fourth century, knew the text and accepted it; their opponents reply that the first Fathers of the Church, like Origen, did not know it and even said that Josephus did not believe Jesus to be the Messiah. Catholics like Mgr Batiffol and Fr Lagrange agree with Guignebert in believing the fragment to be an interpolation, while advanced critics and Protestants like Burkitt and Harnack support its authenticity. Perhaps the best solution is to agree that the paragraph is authentic, but that a Christian copyist added the italicized phrases in order to improve the testimony. The whole question is still undecided.

If we reject these ten lines, the silence of Josephus is impressive. Without going so far as to say with Pascal that "Josephus conceals his nation's shame" (*Pensées*, 629), or as to maintain the paradox that his silence proves the existence of Jesus (for one hates only what exists), we can guess, from our knowledge of the man, why he kept silence. A Jew, who wrote books which were all destined to exalt or defend his people in the eyes of the great Roman public, who says as little as possible about Messianism, an idea which the conquerors held eminently suspect, who could so well paint the essentials of Judaism in the colours of the surrounding paganism—was such a man going to report this incident of a fanatic who had deceived some poor men, disturbed for a time the established order and ended as he deserved, ridiculed and miserable?

These are positively all the documents left us by both pagans and Jews about Jesus and his story. If we did not possess the Christian documents, what should we know of him and his message? But the Gospel is there, one and unimpeachable in its four books. It is the most solid foundation of all our knowledge of the historical Christ and his teachings.

CHAPTER III

WHAT THE DEAD SEA SCROLLS TELL US ABOUT JESUS

By Jean Daniélou, S.J.

The question of the relations between the Qumran manuscripts and the origins of Christianity has many aspects. It is possible that John the Baptist was in touch with the Essene monks, in whose neighbourhood he baptized. In addition, literary parallels have been observed between the New Testament writings, especially those of St Paul and St John, and the manuscripts discovered at Qumran. Finally, as I have shown elsewhere,[1] the ancient non-canonical Christian literature in its turn has characteristic Essene traits. The question we wish to discuss here is: what may be learned from the Qumran manuscripts about Jesus.

That Christ had contacts with the Essene community of his time seems obvious when we remember those he had with John the Baptist after his baptism. But there is an episode which is very significant in this connection: the Temptation. Matthew writes that Jesus was led away by the Spirit into the wilderness, to be tempted there by the devil (Matt. 4. 1). In the absence of other indications, the wilderness, in the context of this incident, seems to mean the region where the Essenes lived. The traditional scene of the Temptation, moreover, is on the cliff where the manuscripts were found, a

[1] *Théologie du Judéo-Christianisme* (Desclée, 1958).

little to the north of Qumran, so that Christ's sojourn in the desert seems to have taken him into the neighbourhood of the Essenes. Even the theme of the Temptation itself reminds us of the Qumran monks: they believed, as the foundation of their doctrine, that man was subject to the rival influences of the devils and the angels, and we are told that Christ was tempted by the devil and afterwards ministered to by angels (Mark 1. 13).

Further, according to St John, the first actions of Christ's public life took place near the mouth of the Jordan. It was there that he recruited his first disciples, who appear to have been followers of John the Baptist, and were expecting the imminent coming of the Messiah. One of Christ's disciples, St John, seems to be very strongly marked in his outlook by the ideas of Qumran: one is tempted to think that he was an Essene. In any case, as Cullmann has shown, the Baptist's disciples formed a connecting link between the men of Qumran and the disciples of Christ.[2] This is confirmed by the fact that Christ's attitude to the Jewish sects agrees with John's. The Essenes are never named in the Gospel, and the reason may well be that in the eyes of Christ they correspond to the "true Israelites", "the poor of Israel".

Having said this, we can discover other traces of contact between the world of Qumran and that in which Christ recruited his disciples. In the first place it is possible (and this is a very remarkable point) that Jesus and his disciples followed the Qumran calendar.[3] It is well known that one of the most difficult problems of New Testament exegesis is to determine the day of the Last Supper. The synoptic Gospels make it a Passover meal and place it on the 14th of Nisan (March-April) in the evening. But for St John the Crucifixion

---

[2] "The Significance of the Qumran Texts for Research into the Beginnings of Christianity", *Journal of Biblical Literature*, 74, 1955, p. 219.

[3] A. Jaubert, "La date de la dernière Cène", *Revue de l'histoire des religions*, 1954, pp. 140–76.

took place before the Passover, in which case Christ was crucified during the day of the 14th Nisan and instituted the Eucharist on the evening of the 13th. In this case the Supper was not a Passover meal, which contradicts the synoptics, unless Christ anticipated the Passover. How can we explain it?

The problem could be solved if it could be shown that at that time there were two different dates for the celebration of the Pasch. Now there exists an old tradition that Christ ate the Passover on Tuesday night, was arrested on Wednesday and crucified on Friday. Hitherto this tradition has been neglected. But Mlle Jaubert has shown that the men of Qumran used an ancient priestly calendar of 364 days to the year, containing four quarters of 91 days, each formed of thirteen weeks. According to this calendar, as the year contains exactly fifty-two weeks, the feasts necessarily fall always on the same day of the month and week. Now in this calendar the Passover was always on a Wednesday, and its eve was therefore on Tuesday. Thus Christ would have celebrated the Supper on the eve of the Passover according to the Essene calendar. But he would have been crucified on the day of the official Passover, which in that year fell on a Friday.

The calendar question is not the only one which suggests a connection between the Supper and the circles of Qumran. Analogies can be seen in the actual institution of the Supper. Matthew writes: "While they were still at table, Jesus took bread, and blessed, and broke it, and gave it to his disciples, saying, Take, eat, this is my body. Then he took a cup, and offered thanks, and gave it to them, saying, Drink, all of you, of this; for this is my blood, of the new testament..." (Matt. 26. 26-7). The essential elements, of course, the transformation by Christ of the bread and wine, and the bond between the blood of Christ and the new covenant, have no parallels in the Essene texts, but the actual arrangement of the Supper, on the other hand, recalls the meals at Qumran. "When they prepare the table for eating and the wine for drinking, the priest shall first stretch out his hand to bless the choice portion of the bread and the wine" (*DSD*, 6, 3–6). These customs, however, were common to the Essenes and other Jewish communities, and it cannot be stated as certain that Jesus borrowed them from Qumran.

There is something stranger still. In one fragment, the messianic meal is described: "When they shall meet at the Table of the Community or to drink wine, and when there is an arranging of the Table and a service of the wine, no one shall stretch out his hand to the choice portion of the bread or the wine before the priest, for he it is that blesses the choice portion of the bread or the wine, and he shall stretch out his hand to the bread first" (IQSa, 2, 17–20). We are reminded of Christ's words: "The hand of my betrayer rests on the table, at my side" (Luke 22. 21). So it seems specially clear that Christ's action shows him to be the expected Messiah and Priest.

Hence there are some who think that the community formed by Christ and his disciples reveals some analogies with the Qumran community. This impression is strengthened by other features. On the one hand Christ established a group of twelve apostles as supreme council of the community he founded. This is obviously an allusion to the twelve sons of Jacob, heads of the ancient Israel, and Christ thus signifies that he is founding a new Israel. But there is perhaps a closer context. It is remarkable that at the head of the Qumran community there was a council of twelve members and three priests. It is hard to say whether the three priests are to be counted among the twelve, but if they are, the connection would be even more striking, since among the twelve apostles there was a privileged group of three, Peter, James and John.

We must add that the manner in which the community's council is described is remarkably like what the New Testament says about the twelve. We read in the Rule: "The council of the community shall be established as an eternal plant, a sanctuary for Israel, as witnesses of the Truth in

view of the Judgement. It is the tried wall, the precious
corner-stone; its foundations shall not shake and shall not
be overthrown" (*DSD*, 8. 4–8). We can find equivalents for
almost every one of these expressions in what Christ says
about the apostles. "You shall also sit there upon twelve
thrones, ... and shall be the judges over the twelve tribes
of Israel" (Matt. 19. 28). The image of the precious corner-
stone, taken from Isaias 28. 16, is also used by Christ, but
applied to himself.

It will be noticed that this enables us to clear up an important point. It has often been held that the organization of a
hierarchy was a secondary element in the Church, one not
originating from Christ, who did not want to found a society,
because, it is thought, he believed the end of time to be at
hand. It is clear, on the contrary, that our Lord's organization
of a hierarchy appears to be rooted in the very milieu in
which he lived. We can also see how little contradiction there
is between the idea of forming this society and that of an
imminent end of time, for the Qumran community, who also
believed in this imminence, likewise founded a society.
And this equally shows that the models which inspired the
structure of the Church are not to be sought in the Hellenistic
world, but in the world of Palestinian Jewry.

Another point concerns the disciples whom Jesus sent
into the towns and villages to preach his message. We remember his charge: "You are not to carry purse, or wallet,
or shoes. ... When you enter a house, say first of all, Peace
be to this house" (Luke 10. 4). Now we read in Josephus
about the Essenes: "They travel, carrying nothing except
arms against robbers. In each town, someone is specially
appointed to receive them as guests" (*Jewish War*, 2, 8, 4).
A similar allusion to the arms occurs in the Gospel. At the
moment when Christ was about to be arrested, Peter said:
"See, Lord, here are two swords", and Christ replied: "It is
enough" (Luke 22. 38). This does not mean that Christ's
disciples were attached to the insurgent Zealots, as Brandon

has said,[4] but simply that, as they had to travel about in a lawless country, they had to provide themselves with the bare means of security.

It is not only in the structure of the hierarchy that we find analogies between the two communities. A curious text shows a resemblance in the organization of the Christian community itself. In the story of the multiplication of the loaves, as told by Mark, we see Jesus commanding his disciples "to sit down in companies on the green grass, and they took their places in rows, by hundreds and fifties" (Mark 6. 39–40). Now the *Rule of the Community* says: "The people shall march in order, in their thousands, their hundreds, their fifties and their tens" (2. 20–2). No doubt this grouping was that which the community specially observed at their annual general assembly on the Feast of Weeks. The analogy is therefore surprising. Yet it must be added that this was the ancient arrangement of the people in the time of Exodus (18. 21–5). Here, too, we find ourselves in a setting which is traditional rather than specifically Essene.

Besides these analogies as to customs, we note that in Christ's discussions with the representatives of the Jewish sects, Pharisees or Sadducees, the positions he adopts are often similar to those of the Essenes. Thus the *C D C* (*The Zadokite Fragment*) forbids all kinds of oaths (15, 1–3). The same thing is found in the Sermon on the Mount: "But I tell you that you should not bind yourselves by any oath at all" (Matt. 5. 34). We notice also the same condemnation of the custom of the Corban, the factitious consecration of an object to God, to avoid having to give it to someone (Mark 7. 11; *C D C*, 16, 14). In all this, Christ appears to endorse the Essene criticism of the Pharisees' casuistry. This always brings us back to the same milieu, one which is opposed both to the Pharisees, by its attachment to tradition, and to the Sadducees, by its spiritual rigorism. But this milieu is cer-

[4] *The Fall of Jerusalem and the Christian Church*, p. 103.

tainly wider than the community of Qumran, which is one of its centres.

A very interesting point of agreement is found in the attitude to divorce, for there is an analogy in the actual terms. We read in *C D C*: "One of the snares is fornication, marrying two wives, each being alive, whereas the *principle of creation* is: male and female created he them" (4, 21). Now we read in Mark: "It was to suit your hard hearts that Moses wrote such a command as that: God, *from the first days of creation,* made them man and woman" (10. 6). The resemblance is so striking that this text is one of those on which J. L. Teicher relies to show that the *Damascus Document* is Judaeo-Christian.[5] This is inadmissible, but the fact remains that in both cases there is the same condemnation of divorce as a corruption contrary to the primitive order.

Certain of Christ's attitudes thus present some analogies with the Qumran community. Must we then conclude that he was an Essene, at least at some period of his life? Here historians are unanimous in affirming the contrary. There is nothing, either in his origins or in the setting in which he habitually lived, to justify such a conclusion. The resemblances we have noted are striking, but not decisive. If the points we have noted are in fact found both among the Essenes and among the disciples of Christ, nothing indicates that they were peculiar to the Essenes. The priestly calendar is also found in the *Book of Jubilees* and in *I Enoch*, which are certainly not Essene; the community meals or *chaburoth* existed elsewhere.

While the resemblances are thus seen to be very external, the differences of attitude, on the other hand, are astounding. The Essenes were very attached to legal observances: in this respect they were more meticulous than the Pharisees. In the observance of the sabbath, for instance, they forbade not

---

[5] "Jesus' sayings in the *DSS*". *Journal of Jewish Studies* (1954), v, p. 38. See also David Daube, *The New Testament and Rabbinic Judaism*, pp. 71–85.

only work, but speaking about one's work (*C D C*, 10, 19); it was forbidden to walk more than a thousand cubits (500 yards) (10, 21), to prepare any food (10, 22), to move stones or earth (11, 1). In this connection we have a specially interesting case, for it is mentioned in the Gospel. We know the question put by Christ, after healing the man with dropsy on the sabbath, to the great scandal of the Pharisees: "Is there any one of you who will not pull out his ass [but many texts read: *son*] or his ox immediately, if it falls into a pit on the sabbath?" (Luke 14. 5). This implies that this was permitted by Pharisaic observance. But this very case is raised in the *Damascus Document*, and is answered in the negative: "If a human being falls into a pool of water, let no man draw him out with a ladder or a rope" (11, 16).[6] "If a beast fall into a well, let no man draw it out on the sabbath" (11, 13).

Now if we compare Christ's attitude to legal observances with this, we find it is the complete opposite, and that on two levels On the one hand he asserts the primacy of charity over legal observances, which scandalizes the Pharisees and, all the more, the Essenes. To give only one example, we think of the passage in which Jesus was passing through a field on the sabbath day with his disciples, and being hungry, they picked the ears of corn and ate them. Seeing this the Pharisees said: "Look, thy disciples are doing a thing which it is not lawful to do on the sabbath." To which Christ replied: "If you had found out what the words mean, It is mercy, not sacrifice, that wins favour with me, you would not have passed judgement on the guiltless" (Matt. 12. 2-7). Charity thus takes precedence of legal observances. But there is more to it. For Jesus adds: "The Son of man has even the sabbath at his disposal." Here is an affirmation unprecedented in its bearing, with implications of which we shall have more to say.

[6] But T. H. Gaster interprets in the contrary sense: *Scriptures of the Dead Sea Sect* (London, 1957), p. 87, n. 54.

Another point on which Christ is radically opposed to the Essenes is the concept of legal purity, especially in the matter of meals. We are struck by the scandal caused by Christ when he eats with publicans and sinners. When the Magdalene approached him, at his supper with Simon the Pharisee, Simon said to himself: "If this man were a prophet, he would know who this woman is who is touching him" (Luke 7. 39). But if this action scandalized a Pharisee, it would have appeared even more scandalous to an Essene. To be admitted to their meals, a man had to serve a novitiate of two years, and even then every meal had to be preceded by an ablution in the tanks, which have been discovered, and a change of clothes. As Lohmeyer has remarked, nothing could have been more revolutionary from the Essene point of view than the fact that Christ ate with the impure and entered the house of a pagan, like the centurion. We should have to consider also the meaning of this revolutionary act. We have only to note it to show how completely the group of Christ's disciples must have differed from the exclusiveness of the men of Qumran.

This contrast is even more striking when we compare Jesus with the most important figure in the world of Qumran, the Teacher of Righteousness. The greater he appears to us when we consider him in himself, the greater appear the differences when we compare him with Christ. No doubt there are certain analogies: each was persecuted by the high priests, but that is something common to many prophets. One may also find resemblances which stem from the religious language of the time. But on the other hand, differences appear even on the most external level. M. Dupont-Sommer has pointed out, in his *Nouveaux Aperçus*, that the Teacher of Righteousness is a priest, but Jesus is "Son of David"; the one is an esoteric teacher, the other a popular preacher.

If we look deeper, the contrasts are more glaring. "No text", writes Millar Burrows, "gives any ground for saying that the Teacher of Righteousness was regarded as the

Messiah." What is called the Messianism of the Qumran documents is simply the importance attached in them to the coming, and that imminently, of the Messiah. But the claim of the New Testament is not merely that the last times are near, but that the event which inaugurates them is accomplished in Christ, who is the expected Messiah, and with whom the Kingdom of God has come, the Judgement has been given, the Resurrection is present, Paradise is opened. The Good News is not that the Messiah is about to come, it is that the Messiah has risen from the dead. In the Teacher of Righteousness what matters is his message; in Christ it is his works of salvation.

In the second place, one of the most remarkable features of the Teacher of Righteousness (if we accept the *Hodayoth* as his work) is the vivid sense he has of being a sinner, and his desire for purification. In this he recalls the noblest psalms of the Old Testament, especially the *Miserere*. But, as has often been remarked, one of the most extraordinary traits in the person of Christ is that we never find him remotely conscious of being a sinner. This is not only in explicit words ("Which of you accuses me of sin?"), but in the whole texture of his conduct. If in others the sense of sin is the hallmark of truly religious souls, so that its absence is always suspect, its absence in Jesus, in whom all recognize a religious quality above all comparison, is an extraordinary enigma.

Thirdly, another trait we find in the Teacher of Righteousness is his awareness of the infinite distance which separates him from God, and it is this which gives his words such a profoundly religious tone. Now if there is one certain fact in the story of Christ, it is that, not only by his words but by his whole behaviour, he claimed divine prerogatives. Apart from this, the Gospel is inexplicable. In fact it was because of this claim that he was accused of blasphemy and finally condemned. "Who can forgive sins, but God, and God only?", asked the Pharisees, proving that in their eyes Christ's action in forgiving sins amounted to claiming divine authority, a claim on the part of a man which to the Jews was the most heinous of crimes. It is the direct opposite of the attitude of the Teacher of Righteousness. There is no better evidence that Christ thus affirmed his divine nature.

Finally, not only was the first Christian community centred on the death and resurrection of Christ as the supreme event of history but it made Christ himself the object of its worship, giving him the divine title of *Kyrios* (Lord). Now there is not the slightest indication that the person and deeds of the Teacher of Righteousness held any such place in the Essene community. Cullmann has remarked that Philo and Josephus are able to give accounts of Essene doctrine without even mentioning the Teacher of Righteousness. We cannot imagine such a thing in connection with the Christian faith. Moreover, the very idea of worship offered to the Teacher of Righteousness at Qumran is unthinkable. He is a prophet honoured after his death. He is the support, not the object, of their faith.

CHAPTER IV

THE GOSPEL: BASIS OF ALL OUR KNOWLEDGE OF JESUS

by Daniel-Rops

THE GOSPEL IS THE LIFE AND THE MESSAGE OF CHRIST

Long before it became that great leather-bound volume carried around by the altar-boy, the Gospel was a spoken word. It was spoken, repeated, recited, for men to whom it brought a revelation, by men who had devoted their whole lives to the task of handing it on. In very truth, this direct message, this eternally overwhelming news, is something we must never allow to become buried under the dust of routine and mumbling monotony; we must ever be recovering that trembling expectation, that fresh and devouring curiosity which, when to belong to Christ was fraught with peril, made those who gave themselves to him his loving slaves. That word of God, which knocks at our hearts during those brief minutes while a curate is reading, moderately well, a score of verses—we must try to hear it falling into the midst of one of those communities of Syria, Asia Minor or Greece, where among the dockers, artisans and shopkeepers some messenger had arrived from Jerusalem or Antioch, and they would listen to him for hours, as men do now to the street story-tellers in Moslem lands. Or again, in one of those secret gatherings, where the same words sounded through the stuffy air of a catacomb, to men and women who, only to hear them, risked the cross, the wild beasts or the fire. For these men and women, the Gospel was indeed news, the most important news of all, the Good News.

The word *gospel*, from the Old English *gód spel*, "good news", translates the Greek *evangelion* and Latin *evangelium*. The verb *to evangelize* had an ancient and solemn meaning with religious associations. When victory had crowned the armies, the herald ran to bring the *evangelium*. At Rome, the era of peace introduced by the accession of Augustus, after so many years of turmoil and suffering, seemed so marvellous that the birth of the Emperor had been proclaimed as an *evangelium*, a "good news".

For an Israelite, what could this "good news" mean? It could only be that which for two thousand years had sounded on the lips of the Chosen People, that which Abraham, Moses, David and the Prophets had uttered, man's calling on God, his praise and thanksgiving. It could only mean that great hope which had filled the Hebrew soul through the ages, the hope of seeing the Kingdom of the Father established on earth, and the Messiah, his son, applying the Law. The "good news" which had sprung from that Palestine trodden by Jesus, and still more that little corner of the world where his cross had been planted, where his wounded body had mysteriously risen from the tomb, had then a double significance. It applied both to the person of him in whom the hope was incarnate, and to the fulfilment which his message had given to the Law of the Lord. In the earliest Christian communities there was only this to be said: "The Messiah has come: he was called Jesus; he did this and that; he saw this and that. We, who are telling you, are his witnesses. Believe in him!" Two thousand years have gone by since these things were said, but what, in substance, has been added to them?

The Gospel, then, was, as it still is, a spoken word. In

actual practice, it was also as a spoken word that it was
elaborated. To understand this, we must rid ourselves for
the moment of our habits as modern men, men of a paper
civilization. For us, reading and writing are two such auto-
matic operations that we can scarcely imagine how some
societies have almost managed to do without them. Our
memories, in consequence, have become anaemic and stiff, but
it is not so among many eastern peoples who make more
demands on it; it was not so in the time of Christ. To learn
by heart and recite were the two normal operations for the
transmission of a text. The great *writers* of Israel were no
doubt, quite literally, great *speakers*; thus the prophecies of
Jeremias were *spoken* over a period of twenty-two years before
being written down. Later, in the same way, the Mishna, the
most essential part of the Talmud, was only written down
after centuries of oral transmission. "A good disciple", said
the rabbis, "is like a well-built cistern: he does not let fall
one drop of water from his master's teaching." We must
imagine the first instruction in the Gospel in the same fashion;
what the apostles stored up in their memory, they taught in-
fallibly to their own disciples, who in their turn would repeat
it to their hearers.

This transmission by memory and the spoken word was,
of course, greatly facilitated by the very technique which
was applied to it. There existed an art of learning and retaining by heart which was part and parcel of an art of
speaking and transmitting: it is what is called the oral style,
found in all human societies where memory plays an important part. The balance of rhythm, the repetition of certain
words, the play of alliterations and rhymes are powerful aids
to memory. In countless passages of the Gospel the traces
of this oral style show through the written text. One has
only to read aloud certain groups of verses to be convinced
by experience:

> We have piped to you, and you have not danced;
> We have lamented and you have not wept.

We are here visibly in the presence of a rhythmical fragment, a genuine refrain.

It is, then, under this form that we must visualize the very first "gospel", something which had to partake of recitation, and also of the popular story, necessarily somewhat schematized and largely artificial in its expression, for it was a matter of instruction which had to be easily remembered. There can be no doubt that the first three Gospels, Matthew, Mark and Luke, the "synoptics", were based on these elements. It is also very probable that before long—and especially when the peculiarly Jewish elements of the original Christian Church were surpassed in importance by the Gentile converts, ignorant of the arts of the oral style—these statements of the oral teaching were supported and stabilized in short summaries or memoranda, which the preachers of the Good News carried about with them, and which are no doubt alluded to in the short prologue to St Luke's Gospel. This stage must have coincided with the change of language: the first apostles, like St Peter, certainly taught in Aramaic, their mother-tongue, the language of Christ, far more than in Greek, though they must have spoken this to some extent. When the first deacons were appointed—all Jews from Greek countries, "Hellenists", as they were called —they normally expressed themselves in Greek. So a Greek Gospel tradition grew up, almost simultaneously with the primitive Aramaic tradition, and it was from this that our written Gospels eventually emerged.

But, whether in Aramaic or in Greek, we must not underestimate the importance of this direct oral transmission of the Gospel. The first Christian generations, those which lived sixty, eighty, or even more years after the death of Christ, attached immense value to it. Suppose that a child of today were told by his grandmother that her own grandmother had told her, when she was a little girl, about Napoleon, how she had seen a review of troops march past, just before Waterloo. Would not this direct memory, this in some sort immediate contact, seem far more concrete, more vivid, truer, than anything he could read in his school history-book? For at least four or five generations, Christians heard the Gospel communicated by word of mouth, by irrefutable witnesses. About 130, when the four evangelists had long ago published their books, Papias, bishop of Hierapolis in Phrygia, declared that what he valued above all, in the matter of tradition, was the "living and permanent voice". He tells how, whenever anyone arrived who had been in direct touch with the "elders", the first disciples of the apostles, all crowded eagerly to hear him. And a little later, in the same way, St Irenaeus, bishop of Lyons, recalls the time when he heard St Polycarp, the great bishop of Smyrna, telling what he had himself remembered of St John. Here we can feel the human warmth, the very truth of life; when, much later, the written text was definitely imposed, after being long concurrent with the spoken word, can we imagine that in these conditions the two could have differed? The written text preserves, for all who can hear, the moving accent of those living testimonies.

Little by little, the witnesses of Christ had died; first those who had seen him with their own eyes, then the disciples, who had heard the apostles speaking of him. The Church was now already powerful, grounded on the living message of the "permanent voice". But the revelation of Christ, being thus handed on without visible, material support—and especially in circles where the art of faithful memorizing was no longer so perfect—ran the risk of being dangerously modified. Deviations or errors might creep in. Some might claim to be more fully possessed of the truth than others: some might assert that they were in the secret of a knowledge —*gnosis*—unknown to others. Against this danger the only possible defence was a written text, unanimously accepted. Now this text existed: about the middle of the second century the Church became sharply aware of the exceptional importance of this fact, aware that by inspiring men to write under the guidance of the Holy Spirit, Providence had provided for everything. The oral tradition could disappear; the written documents were there, already time-honoured and reliable, admitting neither increase nor diminution.

How and when were they composed? In very diverse circumstances, certainly, but all the records of the Good News were alike in being connected directly with the apostles. As St Justin, the martyr teacher, had said, they were "Memoirs of the apostles". One apostle wrote in a Jewish milieu, for men of Jewish upbringing; this was Matthew, the former publican Levi, whom Jesus had called from his customs-office. Another, probably quite a young man who had seen Christ, and in any case had lived in close association with the prince of the apostles, reported what Peter had told him; his name was Mark. A third, Luke, a physician of Hellenic origin, who had followed the great missionary St Paul in many of his journeys, put together what his master had known and also many direct testimonies, through the contacts he had been able to make with the friends and relations of Jesus, and he wrote all this down for the special benefit of the "Gentiles" converted by his master. All this happened within thirty or forty years after the death of Christ. Much later, another apostle, John, the youngest and the most loved by Christ, after a long life of meditation, experience and prayer, resolved to supplement, before he died, the three documents already known, emphasizing the strictly spiritual aspects of Christ's teaching and mission on earth; this fourth document appeared at Ephesus in Asia Minor, about the year 100.

We have only to recall briefly how these texts saw the light of day in order to understand at once the authority they quickly acquired. It was no longer the oral tradition, yet it was the same thing, a tradition as living, as directly linked with the Master, now fixed in final terms. Those who read them could recognize in this or that passage what they might have heard from the lips of the "speakers" of the Good News: they could even discover, no doubt, fragments of those "memoranda" used by the catechists. With these texts, no deviation was now possible. In that vital period of the mid-second century, when the Church effected, so to speak, the synthesis of her truths in view of a decisive expansion, these writings appeared to her, as indeed they were, fundamental.

These writings thus played a determining part in the Christian life, for all Christians knew them to be the direct expression of the message of Christ. The Good News, which Jesus himself is, and which he has brought into the world, is here perfectly transmitted, in a definitive form. And so all these texts are themselves called by the same name which describes the wonderful tidings; they are the Gospel. There is only one, only one Good News, expressed in different forms, but only one nevertheless. St Irenaeus spoke very accurately of the tetramorphic Gospel, the Gospel, that is, which is under four forms. And from the middle of the second century, with Clement of Alexandria and the Muratorian Canon, it was the practice—and the only right practice—to say, the Gospel *according to* St Matthew, *according to* St Mark, *according to* St Luke, *according to* St John, to make it clear that here is a body of truth, substantially one and unique, communicated to men in different modes.

Why was it that, when the Church became conscious of the importance of these texts, she did not try to reduce them to unity by merging them into one? Why did she not do this, in particular, with the first three, whose resemblances make us call them, precisely, "synoptics"? There were essays in this direction, one at least of which, that of the Assyrian Tatian, a pupil of Justin, was composed with very great skill and quickly became popular in the Syrian Churches. Perhaps she knew, with her marvellous sense of reality, that the small differences between the texts, so far from prejudicing their credibility, would strengthen it.[1] And above all, with her profound respect for tradition, she knew she had not the right to make any alterations in documents which derived directly from the first witnesses.

So it was these four texts we know, our four "Gospels", which were recognized as constituting the very foundation of the Christian truths. In a famous passage of his book *Against the Heretics*, St Irenaeus writes: "We do not know the plan of our salvation through any others than those through whom the Gospel came to us: that which they then preached they later handed on to us, by the will of God, in the Scriptures, to be the foundation and pillar of our faith." Why was there such insistence on <u>the number of four</u>? The Fathers of the Church, headed by St Irenaeus, were sure that there were symbolic intentions: four, like the regions of the world, like the chief winds, like Ezechiel's symbolical figures which later inspired the representations of the four living creatures. It is perhaps better to see in this limitation the proof of the care with which the Church chose the texts which should be the "foundation and pillar of our faith".

One appreciates even better the Church's wisdom and prudence on becoming acquainted with the medley of texts which proliferated during the early centuries, all claiming to spring from the most august traditions, but which were rejected by the Church. They are called the *apocryphal gospels*, and some of them had a great vogue in certain parts of Christendom. Many of them do no more than embellish the genuine facts with fables and old-wives' tales, *deliramenta*, as St Jerome calls them. Others reveal more suspicious intentions, for as doctrinal deviations, "heresies", appeared very early in the Church, there was a temptation to try to support them with

---

[1] See below on the synoptics. It should be remembered that the Gospels reflect three historical levels: the sayings and doings of Jesus; the liturgical, doctrinal and apologetic concern of the Christian community decades after Christ; the theological purpose of the author (*Editor*).

texts alleged to be genuinely apostolic. The Church avoided these snares. She retained only those texts which enjoyed the practically unanimous trust of the Churches and could exhibit the guarantee of apostolic origin or approval as proof of their inspired character, and she rejected all the rest.

Thus the Canon came to be fixed. An eighth-century manuscript, called the Muratorian Canon after the collector who discovered it in 1750 at Milan, gives the list of the texts admitted as inspired by the Roman Church about 180, and explains in detail how the choice was made.[2] It proves that by the end of the second century our four Gospels were the only ones reckoned canonical, and it fully confirms the claim that from the beginning of the Good News, that is, from when Christ lived and taught, down to these four precious texts, the connecting thread is unbroken. Through all the words of our "Gospels", it is still really *the Gospel*, the Good News of Christ, and that alone, which we hear.

That is the supreme fact dominating the whole history of the origins of Christianity, and indeed all Christian history: the certitude that we possess the message of Christ himself, communicated to us in a manner which is irrefutable. This certitude is again confirmed by a concrete fact which concerns the actual transmission of these documents. To grasp the importance of this argument it must be remembered that before the invention of printing a text could only be transmitted by successive copyings, and therefore the chances of possessing it exactly, completely free from copyist's errors, diminished as time went by and repetitions increased. It is not generally known that with the great classics the lapse of time between their composition and the earliest surviving manuscripts is nearly always very considerable: fourteen centuries for the tragedies of Sophocles, and as much for Aeschylus, Aristophanes and Thucydides; sixteen centuries for Euripides and Catullus; thirteen for Plato, twelve for Demosthenes. Terence and Virgil are fortunate, the interval

[2] See below, on the texts of primitive Christianity.

being only seven centuries for the former, four for the latter. Now for the Gospels the situation is infinitely better: the two oldest Codices of the New Testament, the *Vaticanus* (in the Vatican) and the *Sinaiticus* (in London) are dated without dispute in the fourth century, which leaves a maximum gap of three centuries between the composition and the manuscripts. But better still: the sands of Egypt have yielded up, and are still often yielding, papyrus writings which have now been dated by archaeologists. For the last thirty years, discoveries of this kind have revealed numerous papyri containing passages of the Gospels, the Egerton papyri, the Chester Beatty papyri, and especially the most famous and precious of all, the minute papyrus fragment of the Rylands Library at Manchester—a few square centimetres —which goes back to the first half of the second century and contains parts of verses of the eighteenth chapter of St John's Gospel. The Bodmer papyri, discovered in 1956, date from the end of the second century and give the greater part of St John and some passages of St Luke. No text of antiquity can produce such a guarantee of authenticity: under the glass case at Manchester what we see is almost the apostle's handiwork, in its very form.

Is this mere chance? No; it is the proof of the primordial importance of the Gospel in the development of Christianity and its expansion. Very early, about the middle of the second century, it became the custom to read passages from it during the Church's chief rite, the *synaxis*, the celebration of the Supper. St Justin says so explicitly, and adds that in listening to these texts it is the very voice of God that we hear: "the voice of Christ which has sounded out through the apostles." The four spread everywhere, the Christian communities passed them on to one another, the missionaries took them with them. They were spiritual treasures, living treasures, which the Christians knew by heart, constantly quoted, expounded, applying their precepts to every circumstance of life, wishing to be buried with them—a wish to which we owe these priceless papyrus discoveries. The moral and spiritual life of the early Christians was formed by the Gospel and by it alone; the oldest Christian literature, that of the *Didache* or "Teaching of the Apostles", is simply a transposition and explanation of it. It was by study of the Gospels that the candidates for baptism were prepared for the faith. Its liturgical rôle became ever more important. The holy Book was placed on the altar, "like the Christ-victim himself", St Ignatius said; it was devoutly kissed; from the fourth century, in the East, a candle was lit when the Gospel began to be read, as a sign of joy. It was through the Gospel that Christians really became conscious of that essential truth, that the whole of Christianity is summed up in a profound union with Jesus.

This is a fact of history, the importance of which cannot be sufficiently emphasized. It has been said, and often repeated, that the four Gospels are not history-books, in the sense we give to the word. Fr Huby observes: "The evangelists did not think of writing a biography, as modern man conceives of it, with scrupulous care for chronological or topographical accuracy. They were above all concerned to throw light on the religious value of the life of Jesus by a choice of scenes which conveyed their own teaching." But the fact remains that because we know these four books to be irrefutable documents, because through their pages we hear the actual voice of Christ, they form an immediate bond between him and ourselves, the surest bond of faith. It must also be noted that all who have attacked Christian doctrine have directed their efforts chiefly against them, to relegate them to the level of fables, to contest their dates, to denounce the alleged defects and interpolations of their text. Fr Lavergne has observed that if we compare these three statements: "Louis XVI was beheaded"; "Joan of Arc was burned"; "Jesus was crucified"; the unbeliever considers the first to be historical, the second half historical, half legendary, the third purely hypothetical. For the disciple of Christ, on the other hand, this third statement is a fact, pure and simple, an absolute truth, and it contains for him the whole doctrine of salvation, precisely because it is *true*. In practice, what is the basis of this conviction? The Gospel.

This really fundamental character of the Gospel, as "foundation and pillar of the faith", is what Christians conscious of their religion have never ceased to proclaim, and it is vital to make it real to those who, in our time, have more or less lost the notion of this evidence. In the age of the martyrs, there is widespread evidence to prove how far our brethren of those early days were aware of this dependence of the faith on the Gospel. In the report of the trial held at Carthage in 180, in the reign of Commodus, we see the humble but heroic Christians of Scilli admitting the possession of the sacred texts as the final proof of their "guilt" in the eyes of the Roman Law. Later, in the last persecutions of the fourth century, we hear Agape, Chionia and Irene, the martyr sisters of Salonika, exclaiming: "We choose to suffer all evils rather than surrender the Holy Books", and the African bishop Felix saying likewise: "I would rather be burned than suffer the Holy Scriptures to be burned." These knew that they owed everything to the Gospel, and that a Christian is no Christian without it.

And even more than its permanent relevance, its universality, what strikes us about this presence of the Gospel in the world and in history is what we might call its *timelessness*. In the work of a great thinker, such as Plato, we are led, more or less, to divide it into two parts; one depending on the circumstances in which it was composed, the other in which the genius really stands above time and delivers an imperishable message. With the Gospel, there is nothing of this sort. Everything in it is immediately present. Everything in it sounds to us exactly as it did to its first hearers. We have only to consider the saints who have really left their mark on history: St Bernard, St Dominic, St Ignatius of Loyola, for example; there is nothing in their thought or work which does not proceed directly from the Gospel, nothing which is not its commentary and application. In a way, we may say that all the great saints are contemporary in the Gospel.

Why is this? Because at bottom this loyalty is not given to a text, which the human intellect, however submissive and respectful, might be tempted to discuss and interpret. It is given to a living being, wonderfully present in these short documents, cropping out, as it were, in every verse in all his felt reality, and evoking not only the adherence of the mind but the offering of the heart. That is the great truth which breaks out on us when we open the Gospel, and equally so when we look at Christian history through its heroes and saints. "Ignatius of Loyola", wrote Fr de Grand-maison, "did not love otherwise than Ignatius of Antioch, in spite of the incredible difference between their worlds, their customs and their characters. The young women saints of our days experience the same sentiments as Perpetua and Agnes, Paula and Cecilia. The Negro boy-martyrs of Uganda repeated the very words of the ancient martyrs." It is not a theory or a doctrine which the pages of the Gospel reveal to us: it is—we repeat it: the life and the message of Christ together—a presence, a model, a love.

When St Paul, throughout his untiring journeys, preached the Good News to the peoples of Asia, Greece and Rome, he loved to repeat that the summary of this Gospel—the same that was preached elsewhere by the apostles and their disciples—was contained in the simplest of phrases: "Jesus Christ crucified". Nothing has changed in two thousand years, and for the Christian of today as in the earliest age, it is "Jesus Christ crucified" who is revealed in the four books, complete, trustworthy, inexhaustible.

What, in fact, do we find in the Gospel? First, the strictly historical facts of the life of Jesus. It is almost exclusively from these four short works that we can reconstruct the events from the Nativity to Calvary, any other documents we may try to recover being but crumbs and dust in comparison. The Gospels enable us to trace the life of Jesus, not without hesitation, not without serious rents and gaps in the thread of the narrative, but with a precision and credibility, we must insist, greater than in many biographies of the illustrious men of antiquity.

All through the verses of the sacred text it is indeed a man who is presented to us—a man and not a myth—a man with his definite characteristics, his personal reactions, his emotions, his feelings, and even his moments of violence and anger. Anyone with the least experience of literary work can see at once that the model on whom the evangelists worked was truly a man, a man of flesh and blood, not some imaginary personage. This man appears to us with an incomparable power of truth. The deeds he performs, the words he speaks, belong to him alone; they are unique; we have only to compare the general tone of the Acts of the Apostles with that of any one of the Gospels to realize the difference. No one, not even a saint, not even an inspired writer, is like Jesus.

What is still more striking is that this man irresistibly arouses affection, that he radiates love and attracts it. Many are the unbelievers who, though unable to reach the conclusion of faith, still feel for Jesus an emotion of love and tenderness. One has only to open the Gospel, to read episodes like that of the woman of Samaria or the raising of the young man at Naim, or the grief of Christ at the tomb of his friend Lazarus, and so many others, to experience in the depths of one's being that warmth of love passionately desired by every human soul, that "burning" which the disciples at Emmaus felt in their hearts when Jesus spoke with them. When Mary Magdalene, astounded, murmured "Rabboni", "Master!", when the disciples called Jesus by this name, when the humblest Christian uses it, it is the emotion of love which is uppermost. "Kyrios Christos": that meant "Christ in all, Christ everywhere." For every reader of the Gospel, "Our Lord" is the friend, the best friend, the friend above all

others. We do not need to have read the Gospels very often
to experience the imperious force of that love. "He who loves
father or mother. . . , or his life more than me, is not worthy
of me."

This historical and psychological knowledge of Jesus is, in
itself, a tremendous thing. In a sense, it is certainly true that
it is fundamental, since it gives faith a sure foundation. There
is no firmer buttress to belief than the certainty of the truth:
how many could believe if it were not clear that here is no
collection of fables? And the radiant figure of incarnate love
constitutes the surest argument for that supreme medium of
knowledge which Pascal calls the "heart". Yet these facts
would be of little account, and would often serve only to
satisfy curiosity and sensibility, if something more were not
revealed beyond them. When St Paul speaks of the glorious
prize of the knowledge of Christ, without which there is no
salvation, he means to indicate not only that knowledge which
rests on historical research or psychological insight, but that
which comes from contact with God and is perfected in him.
So it is not only the real Man, radiant with love, that we
see in the Gospels; it is the living God. The biography of
Jesus contained in the four little books is not confined, like
a human biography, between the two dates of his birth and
his death: by the mystery of the Incarnation it plunges into
the secrets of the divine intentions and goes back to the very
moment when, in the beginning of the world, man was bidden
to exist. By the Resurrection, by the promise of the return in
glory and the judgement, it reaches forward across unimagin-
able darkness to the supreme moment of the consummation
of the world.

This presence of the divine in Christ is what the Gospel
makes so marvellously perceptible. It is a constant outcrop-
ping, a sort of transparency. The miracles are there to attest
it for those who have eyes to see and ears to hear, but even
more than the miracles there is that indefinable touch of the
sovereign and the transcendent which breaks out in all the

words, appears in all the deeds of Christ, and is indeed, when all is said and done, the explanation of that unique, exceptional character we recognize in him. To anyone who has meditated at all on the Gospel, there is no mystery so baffling or so exciting as that of the coexistence in Christ of the divine and the human natures. The mind halts on this threshold, forbidden to proceed. But this impression itself is of immense value to faith: it is because it is forced on us, because it is evident that Christ is God, one only God with the Father and the Spirit, that we feel our adherence to him so well-grounded, that we know ourselves to be utterly dependent on him.

The God-Man did not only live: he spoke. The Good News 's not only the certainty of his presence on earth at a given place and time; it is also his message. Here, too, St Paul has said what had to be said. "The Gospel", he wrote to the Romans, "is an instrument of God's power, bringing salvation to all who believe in it." This is what the martyr St Ignatius said, too, in another form, when he declared that it was by the Gospel that he had learned to live as a true disciple of Christ. The Gospel brings a message; it is a doctrine. That is its third fundamental gift: while it places before our eyes the image of the one Model, and enables us in a way to experience the presence of God before us and in us, it gives us instructions, precise, infinitely simple and decisive, which agree in our conscience with those very principles by which we feel ourselves to be human. In the most secular sense of the word, there is no true *humanism* which does not rest on axioms exactly similar to those of the Gospel: the "folly of the cross" and the wisdom of the nations, set out in this little work, are found to be one thing.

That is why we, who listen to the Gospel with the ears of faith, experience not only a twofold sense of love and dependence, but also that reverence, that attentive and eager submission which a disciple gives to his master. The title of *Master*, so often given to Christ, is no courtesy title: it expresses a truth which none can challenge. If all human "mastery" has its limits, Christ's is limitless. The more we study the message of the Gospel and the more we try to deepen our understanding of it, the more clearly we shall see that we cannot exhaust it. A child can grasp its elementary lessons and find them perfectly suited to its childish needs, but there is no metaphysic too profound to find itself there, up to those dizzy heights where the mind of man loses its foothold. And the wonderful thing is that this message is presented in unbroken clarity, never wrapping itself up in those abstract vocabularies and that complicated dialectic used by the philosophers. The mystery in it is truly "full in the light", and the Church, the trustee of this message, has always refused to admit the existence of some esoteric tradition, in rivalry with its clear and universal tradition. And because the message is that of the Man in whom infinite love is incarnate and achieved, it is the most moving that mankind has ever heard, one which in one way or another can always touch every man in his heart.

Biography of the man that Jesus was; revelation in his acts and words of an ineffable Presence; teaching of a doctrine which has never been and never can be equalled in fullness; the Gospel is all that. That is why it surpasses in importance every earthly work and reveals itself as universal and eternal. It is less than the truth to say that it is the news of Christ's coming, the echo of his voice, as one might be tempted to say in order to emphasize its veracity. It is more. The prophets of Israel were only "echoes" of God, and St John was only "a voice crying in the wilderness". The Gospel is more than that. It is that "Word proceeding from silence" of which St Ignatius of Antioch speaks; it is itself "the Word" to which we must submit if we would find salvation. This is the Word which sounds forth and is manifested when, in the humblest village church, three parts empty, a perhaps inattentive priest pronounces the familiar words: "At that time, Jesus said ...". It is enough. Before us stands, as a living presence, that Word who "was made flesh and came to dwell among us", the one Master, the one Model.

THE FIRST GOSPEL:
ACCORDING TO ST MATTHEW

Coming one day out of Capernaum, Jesus saw a customs-officer sitting at his desk. "Follow me!", he said to him, and at once the man followed him. It is by this brief scene, so moving in its simplicity, as we read it in the three synoptic Gospels (Matt. 9. 9; Mark 2. 14; Luke 5. 27), that we know the man whom the Church affirms to be the first evangelist. For him, as for the rest of the twelve, a word was enough: —scarcely even a word; a look or a sign—and at once he left his customs-office, just as Peter, Andrew and John had left their fishing-nets. His name was Levi, the son of Alphaeus. In the college of the apostles, perhaps to mark the break with his old self as a tax-collector, he took the name of Matthew, which means "Gift of God". He was therefore a Jew of Galilee, of a certainly well-to-do class (he offered Jesus a banquet immediately after his call), and no doubt of some education, without which he could not have kept his books and accounts. That is all we know about him.[3]

On what grounds is the first Gospel attributed to this apostle? First, on tradition. The attribution is, in fact, very ancient, since it was current among the Churches at the beginning of the second century. Writing his five books on the *Exposition of the Lord's sayings*, about 120 or 130, Papias, bishop of Hierapolis (who had certainly known at least one of the apostles), asserts that "Matthew set in order the Lord's sayings in the Hebrew language". This indication is confirmed by numerous later testimonies, both implicit, such as those of the *Didache*, the *Epistle of Barnabas*, St Ignatius and St Justin, and explicit, as those of St Irenaeus, Tertullian,

---

[3] There are traditions, of uncertain value, which regard him as the evangelist of Arabia, Ethiopia and even Persia.

Origen, Eusebius and St Jerome. It is beyond question that all Christian antiquity ascribed to St Matthew the glory of being the first of the evangelists, and the unanimity of the tradition is most significant, precisely because this apostle is one of the most obscure. It can only be explained if it conforms to the truth, for if it were only a question of giving the Gospel an illustrious patron, a more imposing name from among the twelve would have been chosen.

Internal criticism—that is, the analysis of its intentions, doctrine and style—fully confirms this attribution. To be convinced that the author was a Jew, addressing Jews, one has only to read his text, once we know anything about Palestine in the time of Christ. Did he not define himself as "a scholar whose learning is of the Kingdom of God" (13. 52)? He is clearly expert in everything concerning the Jewish race and traditions. He alludes to "one jot, one flourish" of the Hebrew alphabet (5. 18). He denounces the quibbles and tricks used to get round the Law of Moses (23). From this point of view, a linguistic detail is very significant: he always uses the expression "Kingdom of the heavens" and not "Kingdom of God", for the rabbis and doctors of later times, in order to avoid pronouncing the ineffable name of the Lord, always substituted for it symbolic terms like the Glory, the Power or the Heavens. It is, then, a Jew, addressing Christians of Jewish origin—and we shall see that his doctrinal intentions, too, envisage this special milieu of the Jewish Christians—who is the author of the first Gospel. There is therefore nothing to prevent us calling him, like Papias, Matthew.

We may now re-examine the indication furnished by the aged bishop of Hierapolis, that "Matthew set in order the Lord's sayings in the Hebrew language". *In the Hebrew language*: this means that the first evangelist at first wrote in Aramaic, the usual tongue of Palestine at that time, and not in Hebrew, the literary and liturgical language, which was no longer used by the people. *Set in order*: the expression

may seem strange at first, but in fact it is perfectly com-
prehensible if we remember the manner in which the Good
News was first preached. When some decades had passed
after Christ, the oral transmission of the stories of his life
and message must have become somewhat anarchical. The
little "memoranda" which circulated were no longer sufficient.
All this had to be classified and arranged: this was the work
of the apostle, of the only apostle, no doubt, who had a
certain literary education, and this was his claim to praise.

At what date was this work carried out? Tradition affirms,
and this is confirmed by the Biblical Commission, that
chronologically the Gospel according to St Matthew was the
first. That it was earlier than 70, the year of the capture
and destruction of Jerusalem by the Roman armies, is obvious,
for he does not mention the fulfilment of Christ's prophecy
on the ruin of the holy City, which he could not have failed
to do if he had witnessed it. A passage of St Irenaeus, bishop
of Lyons, has sometimes caused it to be thought that this
Gospel was composed "when Peter and Paul were founding
the Church in Rome", that is, after the year 61 when Paul
arrived there, but this text is susceptible of various interpretations. Other commentators, relying on the statements of
the historian Eusebius (fourth century), maintain that this
Aramaic Gospel was composed before the apostles left Palestine, that is, before 44, which would date this document less
than fifteen years after the death of Christ. It may therefore
be held for certain that the Aramaic text was in existence
by about 50–55.

But one thing is still more certain, and that is that we
do not possess this primitive text. All the Fathers' quotations
from the first Gospel are taken from a Greek translation,
that of our present Canon. Here Papias again gives us precious
information: he says, in fact, in connection with Matthew's
"setting in order" the Lord's sayings, that "each one translated it as best he could". We can easily understand how this
could have happened. Every bearer of the Good News, when

addressing pagan hearers, used the Aramaic document, but translated it aloud. These translations were no doubt approximate and partial, and the Church preferred to replace them by a definitive text.

Who then undertook this version? We cannot say for certain. It is by no means impossible that Matthew translated his work himself and that his translation won recognition over others. The correct Greek of this translation could, however, have been a translation made by someone else. In any case, when the work was finished, the two other synoptic Gospels were in existence: in these primitive Christian communities, where everything about the Saviour was passionately studied, Luke and Mark were already read, expounded and compared with the old Aramaic text. As in any literary milieu, we must presume that there was a whole complex of actions and reciprocal reactions, and so it is natural to suppose that the translator of the old Gospel, in order to perfect his task, took into account the other documents he had under his hand: this would give rise to certain influences of form, certain harmonizations of one text with another, perhaps a few borrowings. This work must have been finished about 70, forty years after the death of Christ.

When we consider this first Gospel as a whole, we cannot help being struck by its methodical character, very different, for example, from the rich outpourings of St John. Matthew, the revenue official, likes clear expositions, well-made plans, carefully controlled developments. It is certainly not by accident that Papias praises him for "setting in order". The ancients attached great importance to the orderliness—*taxis* —of a literary work, and this discipline of the Greek grammarians was known and practised by the Hellenistic Jews. Moreover, these classical principles of order were readily applied to the literary mnemonic devices so beloved of the Jewish rabbis, to their rhythmical recitations, to their systematic methods of grouping ideas and facts. The total result is a narrative which is didactic indeed, but clear and precise.

The work is planned in four parts (as we shall likewise find in Mark and Luke): the episode of John the Baptist; the preaching of Jesus in Galilee; the journey from Galilee to Jerusalem; the Passion and Resurrection; an order which is certainly chronological, but into which episodes are introduced without excessive thought for their order in time. With a view to good composition, the events are often collected together, but connected by vague formulas. For the discourses of Christ, this is even more marked: all the Lord's sayings are grouped in six developments, each beginning with a set phrase, such as "Afterwards, when he had finished these parables. . . ." It is therefore more than likely that Jesus did not pronounce all at once and in succession those sayings which Matthew reports as following one another. If one compares the first Gospel with St Luke's, one realizes, for example, that the Our Father has been moved to another position for literary reasons of exposition. Again, were the parables which are said to have been given by the shore of the Lake of Genesareth actually spoken all at the same time, or is this a case of systematic grouping? The intention is of course obvious: it is in order to strike home more vividly to men's minds, the better to enable the memory to retain the facts, that the evangelist uses these methods.

Yet this didactic method does not weary us. It is compensated for by sure literary qualities. When he reports Christ's sayings—and this is St Matthew's chief preoccupation—we have a very definite impression that they are transcribed exactly, with minute fidelity: they have nothing in common with those transpositions and commentaries in which the Graeco-Roman historians pretend to report the speeches of their characters. There is also a taste for breadth, magnificence, the hieratical, a constant reference, explicit or implicit, to the Old Testament and its prophecies, which enrich the style, without ever letting it lose a character of simplicity and moderation which is the mark of a great good sense. There is no lack of "local colour" in his expressions,

rendering the primitive Aramaic into Greek: we think of
certain formulas which come from St Matthew, like *the consummation of the world, this adulterous generation, the outer
darkness.*

And yet, we must admit, this writing which is the work
of an apostle, one who had known Jesus so well, does not
give the impression of an eye-witness report. His portrait
of the Lord and of the other apostles has something dry
and schematic about it; it is not fully alive. How far it is
from the nervous sensibility of St Luke! The purely human
aspects of the twelve, which in the other Gospels bring them
so near to us, their lack of comprehension before the mysteries
in which they took part, their sometimes rather mediocre
sentiments of petty ambitions and bitter thoughts—St Matthew
waters them down. There is little or nothing of picturesque
detail. Perhaps this springs from the very nature of the
writer: more "auditive" than "visual", more inclined to report
words than to give a concrete picture of facts! Perhaps, too,
he thinks that for still untaught hearers details are useless,
or perhaps it is that he considers a certain sort of realism
does not suit well with the lofty style he intends to maintain.

On the whole, these purely literary characteristics are just
those we might expect, given the conditions in which this
Gospel was composed. When Matthew was writing his Aramaic text, he was supplying a precise need felt by the Church:
to fix the oral catechesis, to lay down in a document the
more or less scattered elements of the current tradition. This
primitive catechesis inevitably had a character of rather
schematic simplicity, since it was addressed to people who
could supply the concrete details for themselves. For us, reading it after two thousand years, while it has not the expressive
realism of St Mark nor the tender delicacy of St Luke, and
though it does not aspire to the lofty flights and transcendent
meditations of St John, it yet remains the one which is best
for teaching, which best fixes the great facts of the Christian
faith and hope in our minds. "The Gospel of the Lord's

Sayings", as Papias said, "the Gospel of the divine order of the Church", as Fr Allo calls it, is certainly the one which best lends itself to public reading. That is why the Church, in her choice from the four Gospels for reading at Mass, shows a decided preference for it. On nineteen out of the fifty-two Sundays of the year, it is St Matthew who is read to us.

From each of the four Gospels emerges a particular intention, which derives from the conditions in which it was written and the people for whom the evangelist intended it, but reveals, to us, one of the significant aspects of the message of Christ. Writing for Christians of Jewish origin, Matthew explains what most interests them: that is, that Jesus is indeed the Messiah, he for whom all faithful Israelites are waiting, the Son of David, the Lord's Anointed. He begins his book with a specifically Jewish document, the genealogy, demonstrating the Davidic descent of Jesus. In his person, as Matthew never fails to insist, the prophecies are fulfilled: "All this was so ordained to fulfil the word which the Lord spoke . . .", the phrase is repeated constantly throughout his work.[4] Behind the human story of Jesus, it is the divine intention, gradually manifested through the meditation of Israel, that he seeks to bring to light.

The first Gospel is thus above all the Gospel of Messiahship. The Jesus we contemplate, under St Matthew's guidance, is truly the Messiah, the envoy of God, the hope of whose coming had inspired the hearts of Israel, he whom we modern Christians must learn again to expect with unfailing desire. It is (with the fourth) the Gospel which shows the relations between the Old and the New Law: it claims to be the continuation and achievement of all that the holy Book of Israel had taught to men. "Heaven and earth must disappear sooner than one jot, one flourish disappear from the Law. . . ." That

[4] He not only makes connections with the Old Testament which Jesus himself makes, but adds many others, which often seem to us rather far-fetched, in the manner of the doctors of the Law.

loyalty to Israel, to which so many Christians are blind, is a constant implication of St Matthew's text.

But while it affirms Israel's unique glory, that of conceiving and bringing forth the Messiah, at the same time it proclaims Israel's guilt in failing to recognize him. The underlying thought of the whole Gospel is expressed in the sorrowful appeal of the twenty-fourth chapter: "Jerusalem, Jerusalem, how often have I been ready to gather thy children together, as a hen gathers her chickens under her wings; and thou didst refuse it!" It is to this Jewish people, at once predestinated and unfaithful, that the love of the Messiah is offered: was he not sent in the first place to the lost sheep of the house of Israel? Was it not the apostles' first mission to bring the Word to the chosen people, always dear to the heart of God? But since Israel will not accept the light, since it stumbles at the rock of offence, one must separate oneself from those who are to blame: those Pharisees, those fanatics for the Law who withstand the truth; the new wine must not be put in old bottles. This accounts for the repeated violence of the condemnations levelled against them, a violence which the other synoptics, writing for Christians of pagan origin, noticeably tone down, this problem of the relations with Israel being of less direct concern to them.

Another aspect of Christ's message stressed by St Matthew —one closely linked with the Messianic idea—is the Saviour's divine Sonship, a vital point, which has not always been sufficiently prominent in Catholic exegesis, here embarrassed by the comparison with St John. Nonetheless, the first evangelist, like the fourth (although in a different way), most clearly affirms that Jesus is the Son of God. At his baptism, at the temptation in the wilderness, by the words of the possessed, by the witness of the paralysed man whom he healed, by St Peter's confession, by the parable of the murderous dressers of the vineyard and in countless other passages, this divinity of Christ is asserted beyond possibility of debate. Here again appears the Jewish point of view: it is because Jesus proclaimed himself "Son of God" before Caiaphas that he was condemned to death.

This, we may say, is the fundamental element of the first Gospel. But this Jewish character, which might have confined it as in a strait-jacket, tends on the contrary to broaden it. Because the chosen People, trustee of the Promise, has not learned to attend to the signs, because it has been unfaithful, it must break out of its narrow framework. Starting from a strictly Jewish standpoint, the Gospel culminates in the widest possible perspective. We have only to think of the incidents of the centurion (8. 5, 11) and the Chanaanite woman (15. 21, 28), of the parable of the tares (13. 17–40), and above all of the great final command: "Go out, making disciples of all nations" (28. 19), to realize the width of its horizon. St Matthew, moreover, is the only evangelist who names the Church (16. 18; 18. 17), which our Lord clearly asserts to have taken the place of the Synagogue, and says, equally formally, that it is not reserved for the Jews alone but has been opened to all nations. Matthew's universalism, though not as marked as that of Mark and Luke, who were writing to "Gentile" Christians, is perhaps even more touching, for it springs from the sorrow caused to a Jew, aware* of his loyalties, by Israel's decisive refusal.

Thus deeply rooted in the past, and at the same time pointing to the future, this document holds a position of capital importance. It is not only because it was historically the first that St Matthew's Gospel now stands at the beginning of the New Testament: it is also for reasons of logic. The first Christians quoted it with a frequency which may seem surprising[5] if we lose sight of its aspect as a "turning point", as a spiritual hinge. "The Gospel of the Church", as Renan saw it long ago, is that in which perhaps most clearly appears the idea, so dear to St Augustine, that Christianity is a permanent value of the human spirit, developed

[5] One hundred and seventy times by St Justin, the second-century martyr apologist.

according to the divine intention in the course of history, and never ceasing to lead society towards its destiny.

THE SECOND GOSPEL: ACCORDING TO ST MARK

The threads of the web on which the first Gospel is woven are, as we have seen, "the Lord's Sayings". The second, on the contrary, is much less interested in Jesus' discourses, but makes up for this by observing and reporting his actions. It is the observation of his deeds, not the echo of his words. St Mark is Christ's chronicler.

We have here a modest booklet—fifty pages at most, the shortest of the four—filled with stories, anecdotes, little factual incidents. It was far from the author's aim to write a complete biography of Jesus; such an intention was in any case foreign to ancient mentality. In general he certainly follows the four-part division, just like Matthew, but he takes little care to arrange the episodes according to logical sequence, and details of chronology concern him not at all. We are far from the careful ordering of the first Gospel, and Papias does not hesitate to speak of Mark's "disorder".

This apparent disorder, this unrestricted manner, these marks of an actual eye-witness, have provoked unending discussion on the origins and authorship of the second Gospel. Such traits, some say, are surely those of ocular evidence, of a sort of collection of notes taken down from day to day and arranged more or less anyhow. This suggests those memoranda which are suspected to have existed in the primitive catechesis: from there, it is but a step to suppose that this Gospel was the source of the other synoptics. Other exegetes have supposed that the second Gospel was a compilation of incongruous elements, stories and collections of sayings, put together, according to some, by an author: according to others, by the "collective conscience" of the Christian community. To all these hypotheses the Church opposes an affirmation: it attributes the second Gospel to a man called Mark.

For this affirmation there is in the first place an argument from common sense, which Renan himself has brought forward—the same as for Matthew. If this attribution were due to a fraud, why should its originators have selected a character of such secondary importance as Scripture represents St Mark to be, in order to credit him with the authorship of this text? It would have been far more flattering to christen it the "Gospel according to St Peter"! But there is more to be said, if we consider the second Gospel in relation to the others and in itself.

Its literary qualities are revealing. The author is certainly no scholar, no scribe: his language is awkward, scarcely correct; he hardly ever varies his methods of narration. He writes as one might who was a Jew, with a sufficient smattering of Greek to conduct his business, in an age when Greek was the common tongue. And yet this mediocre stylist moulds his style with details, "drawn from the life", as Renan says, with penetrating remarks, subtle allusions; he notices a glance of Christ, reveals his deepest thoughts; he reveals human reactions in his divine Model. If one compares certain episodes in Mark with the same in the other synoptics—the Transfiguration, or the raising of Jairus' daughter, or the episode (3. 7–12) when Jesus was so mobbed by the enthusiastic crowd that he had to board a boat to escape them—one can see how remote are Matthew and Luke from the bold relief of Mark's style. Here, too, the impression is clear: this is the style of a man whose sensitivity was strongly marked, as it is during youth, and who has faithfully recorded his emotions.[6]

Another class of observations may help to make things still clearer. The author of the second Gospel is certainly a Jew, thoroughly conversant with the customs of the chosen

---

[6] The first six chapters are rather different in style from the rest, but not so different as to be ascribed to a different author.

people and its traditions, but it is clearly not to Jews that he is writing. If it were, he would not trouble to say that the Jordan is a river, nor to translate his Aramaic expressions, nor to explain Jewish customs such as the washing of hands before meals, the baths after returning from market, the ritual washing of cups. It has also been remarked that he hardly ever appeals to the argument from prophecy, which Matthew uses so freely, fresh proof that he is not addressing readers of the Law and the Prophets. On the other hand, from examination of his style others have thought that they can detect flagrant Italianisms, words transposed from Latin into Greek, corresponding to Hebrew originals. It is also in Roman money that he transcribes the sums in figures which appear in the Gospel. A typical detail: when he is describing the carrying of the cross, he says that Simon of Cyrene was the father of Alexander and Rufus (15. 21); now St Paul, in the Epistle to the Romans, alludes explicitly to Rufus. The inference is strong that the second Gospel was addressed to Romans, and perhaps it was because his Roman hearers typically preferred action to speeches that he composed his work in the way he did.

To sum up, then; a Jew, who in his youth had lived with the spiritual authorities in the Church, who had been strongly affected by these men's stories, who had retained, as one does at the age of twenty, hundreds of concrete, vivid details and, when he wrote his Gospel, wrote for Christians who were Romans, not Jews: all this fits admirably with what tradition asserts: that this author was Mark.

In the Acts of the Apostles there are several allusions to a certain John, also called Mark (12. 12–25; 15. 37), or to a John (13. 5, 13), or to a Mark (15. 39). A Mark is also mentioned in the Epistles of St Peter (1 Peter 5. 13) and St Paul (Col. 4. 10; Philemon, 24). It is agreed that these texts all refer to one and the same person, who added to his Jewish name of John the Roman "cognomen" of Mark; it is to him that Christian antiquity attributed the second Gospel.

Seen through the medium of these documents, John Mark, when Jesus was alive, was a young man of Jerusalem, whose mother Mary belonged to the band of women who were devoted to Christ. The house of this devout woman was a meeting-place for the first Christians; here Peter took refuge when he was miraculously freed from prison by an angel. Though not a direct disciple of Jesus (he was doubtless still too young), Mark had lived in a circle which was very close to him, and these youthful encounters with the Master marked his life and work for ever after.

The impression left on him by these contacts with Jesus was perhaps even stronger, if it is true, as many have thought, that Mark found himself accidentally involved at close quarters with the drama of the Passion. Describing the arrest of Jesus, the second evangelist gives a detail which he alone provides; when all had deserted the Master, a young man followed him, clad only in a linen shirt; the guards tried to arrest him but he fled, leaving the shirt in their hands (14. 51–2). These two curious verses are a sort of parenthesis in the story, and no other evangelist knows of it. But then if all the witnesses had fled, who could have recorded the scene, if not the one who was the hero of it? The boy, hearing a noise in the garden of his mother's house, slipping outside half dressed in a hastily donned shirt, seeing the soldiery arresting Jesus and nearly being arrested with him—how could he forget this dramatic incident? How could he fail to attach it to the memory of his captive Friend?

Whatever the truth may be about this "signature of humility", whether or not Mark slipped it into his Gospel, like those craftsmen of our cathedrals who hid their names behind the angle of a turret, it is certain that after the Lord's death and resurrection Mark entered the Christian Church. A cousin to St Barnabas, he accompanied him on his mission to Antioch, where he met Paul. On St Paul's first missionary journey he parted company with him and returned to Jeru-salem. This so displeased Paul that he refused to take the young man on his second mission, and Mark followed Barnabas to Cyprus. However, this disagreement was not lasting, for ten years later, in 61–2, we find Mark with Paul, bringing aid to the apostle in prison; the Epistles to the Colossians and to Philemon are sufficient proof that affection between the two was completely restored. It was still stronger between Mark and Peter, for the prince of the apostles, writing from "Babylon" (that is, Rome), sends the greetings of his "son" Mark. Later Mark must have been in Asia Minor, for Paul says to Timothy: "Join company with Mark and bring him here with thee; he can help me with the exercise of his ministry" (2 Tim. 4. 11). Altogether it is obvious that Mark was very closely involved in the beginnings of the Church, and that the documents available to him must have been first-hand.

From the actual evidence of Scripture, it would appear that Mark's relations with Paul were much more numerous than with Peter. Yet the earliest tradition assures us unani-mously that it was Peter's mind he reflected. Had not Peter been the friend, and a very intimate friend, of his mother, since it was in her house that he immediately thought of hiding after his escape from prison? Was it not from Peter's hands that he received baptism, since the apostle calls him his "son"? Here are the words of Papias, bishop of Hierapolis, whose testimony is directly dependent on the tradition of the apostles: "Mark, who had been Peter's interpreter, wrote down accurately, but not in order, all that [Peter] remembered of what the Lord had said or done. For Mark had not heard the Lord, and had not been his disciple, but he had later been Peter's, as I said. Peter used to give his teaching accord-ing to the needs of the moment, without meaning to give the Lord's teachings in order...." This evidence, which is confirmed by several early writers, such as St Justin, St Irenaeus and Clement of Alexandria, represents the second

Gospel as the direct emanation of what Peter taught in his lifetime. It has been noticed that the famous sermon in which Peter summed up the Christian teaching, and won the centurion Cornelius to the faith, is a sort of draft or outline of the second Gospel. Mark, handing on what he had received from this most eminent of witnesses, could record the episodes of the life of Christ with all the bold relief and artless realism of the Galilean peasant.

How was he induced to write down his Gospel, that is, to put together all the memories he had collected? Eusebius of Caesarea, the first Christian historian, quoting the testimony of Clement of Alexandria, says explicitly: "So brightly shone the light of piety in the minds of Peter's hearers, that they refused to be satisfied with a momentary hearing . . . they set about begging Mark (whose Gospel we possess and who was Peter's companion) and urging him to leave them in writing a lasting record of the teaching they had received by word of mouth. They refused to give him any peace till they had got their way." We can therefore visualize exactly the circumstances in which the second Gospel was committed to writing. Mark had joined Peter in Rome; he was his friend, his favourite disciple, his spiritual son; the community of Roman Christians begged him to record the apostle's teaching, and he complied. All the characteristics of his text agree with this explanation, his "disorder", his realism, the Latin influences we have noticed.[7]

At what date was this work done? Obviously, during Peter's residence in Rome, but it may be objected that the dates of that residence are not certainly fixed. Unanimous Catholic tradition affirms that chronologically Mark is certainly the

---

[7] There is a curious detail which shows how fresh Mark's memory must have remained in Rome. In the second century St Hippolytus of Rome speaks of the second evangelist and says he was "stump-fingered". This unexpected observation is proof that the memory of the man had been handed down directly for two or three generations.

second evangelist. If Matthew wrote about 55, then Mark must be dated after that. In any case his text, like Matthew's, is earlier than 70 and the destruction of Jerusalem, for the vague manner in which he reports the great discourse of Christ on the end of the City cannot be a prophecy after the event. On the other hand, as we shall see, it is certainly earlier than Luke. To sum up, then, the most commonly accepted date for the composition of the second Gospel is 55–62. Composition, we say, for certain interpretations of a passage of Irenaeus suggest that he possibly did not publish it at once and that his text did not circulate among the Christians till after the apostles' martyrdom. In any case, it is certain that thirty years after the death of Christ this "chronicle" of his life was being read.[8]

The conditions in which Mark wrote his Gospel explain the essential traits we find in it. As interpreter of the thought of Peter, who had known Jesus so well, he aims above all at depicting Jesus as he was, emphasizing his human nature before all. No other evangelist so well enables us to touch, with our fingers, Jesus, the man. With perfect candour he does not hesitate to reveal certain apparent limitations to his power, as when he writes that in his home country "Jesus could not do any wonderful works" (6. 5), or that Jesus protested when a man called him "Good master", because God alone is good. This absolute truthfulness, by inspiring our confidence, makes still more impressive Mark's moral portrait of Jesus as a man without fault, a model of all the virtues.

But with the same truthfulness, the same simplicity, he records everything about Jesus which reveals the divine power, exactly as the apostles claim to be eye-witnesses of

---

[8] According to traditions echoed by Eusebius and St Jerome, Mark, after his time in Asia Minor, founded the Church of Alexandria. But the Alexandrian doctors, Clement and Origen, are ignorant of this detail, which would have been of great interest to them.

these miraculous events. Mark sets it all down. He even lays special stress on Christ's miracles and sets himself to throw light on them. One feels that he was not unwilling to show the ancient pagans who listened to him that his God was more productive in genuine prodigies than the divinities of the Pantheon in feigned miracles. The Son of God, mighty worker of miracles, conqueror of demonic powers, would appeal much more powerfully than the Messiah of Israel to such an audience.

And so, too, our Lord's messianic character, though not passed over in silence in the second Gospel, is not in the foreground. The ancient pagans could not experience, like the Israelites who heard Matthew, the power of hope contained in the very word *Messiah*. Mark also emphasizes, even more than the other two synoptics, what is called the "messianic secrecy" of Jesus: that is, the reserve he imposed on letting himself be known as Messiah (1. 24, 25, 34, 44; 3. 11–12; 8. 30). Rationalist critics have even adduced Mark in support of their theory that Jesus never proclaimed himself as Messiah, but that he was given this title by the faith of the first generation of Christians, inserting into the story of his life declarations which were purposely gradual, thus giving the story a twist. On the contrary, in fact, it was just because Mark exactly reported the evidence of Jesus' intimates that he was led to report the events in this manner. Peter well knew why it was only gradually that Jesus proclaimed his messianic dignity: it was to avoid seeming to sanction the Jewish idea of a national and political Messiah, and so arousing disturbances which would have drawn down the wrath of the occupying power, and above all to accustom the Jews to the idea of a purely spiritual Messiah, whose task would be accomplished in suffering.[9] There was no real "messianic secrecy"; there was simply, in the intentions of Jesus, which are perfectly visible in the second Gospel, the

[9] St Luke too certainly had a similar intention. Cf. Luke 4. 35, 41; 9. 21.

single desire that the meaning of his message should be rightly understood by his own friends: for example, in the famous scene where he lets Peter proclaim him as Messiah, and immediately afterwards foretells his Passion. The connection is deeply significant.

So we may say that the second Gospel shows us both of the two inseparable faces of the divine figure; the divine and the human; which is to say how precious it is for all who would explore the greatest of psychological mysteries, the co-existence in Jesus of the divine and human natures. There is a further point, of great historical interest. As is only natural, when we remember this Gospel's background, one character, Peter, appears in a privileged light. It is through Mark that we know the prince of the apostles, with his ardent and impulsive heart, his rather presumptuous generosity, his spiritual vigour and his human weakness. The importance of Peter's rôle is constantly emphasized: thus in the story of the Passion, out of the seventy-two verses of Chapter 14, twenty-two refer to him by name. In many scenes, as in that of the Passion or of the denial during Jesus' trial, one has the impression of ocular evidence. But —and this is a striking detail of great psychological interest —while the facts unfavourable to Peter are retained, such as his being reproached by Christ (8. 33; 14. 37), and his lapse (14. 66–72), the points to his credit are passed over in silence; the promise of the primacy, his walking on the water, the coin in the fish's mouth, etc. This attitude, which is confirmed by tradition, convinces us how truly the prince of the apostles was also the humblest of men at heart, so that in his oral teaching he never stressed anything which might have put himself in the foreground. He is the same man who, in the hour of martyrdom, asked to be crucified head downwards, deeming himself unworthy to die in the same manner as his Master.

THE THIRD GOSPEL: ACCORDING TO ST LUKE

If St Mark was St Peter's interpreter, St Luke was St Paul's. Such has been the Church's tradition, since at least the end of the second century. It is affirmed by the Muratorian Canon, a catalogue of the sacred books accepted by the Roman Church about 180, and called after the scholar who discovered it in 1750. St Irenaeus states it formally in the same period. All subsequent evidence repeats this attribution: Luke, author of the third Gospel, the "beloved physician" found following in the steps of St Paul, is that hellenized Oriental who accompanied St Paul in so many of his adventures, the same who later wrote the Acts of the Apostles. Eusebius of Caesarea, the Christian historian of the fourth century, expounds all this in detail.

Further, internal criticism (that is, the examination of the text) provides striking confirmation of the ancient evidence. The identity of the author with the author of the Acts is now scarcely disputed; and in the Acts he places himself so definitely in Paul's train that on several occasions he says "we"; these "we" passages are in a style strictly identical with that of the Gospel. This evangelist, who handles Greek with ease, appears to be a cultivated man, trained in a minimum of scientific method. His relations with St Paul shine out in his vocabulary (seventy-five words have been noted which occur only in St Luke and St Paul), in certain literary similarities, in some doctrinal analogies, especially on the universality of salvation and justification by faith. Luke is of course far from possessing the theological depth of that genius St Paul and is less subject to his master's influence than is St Mark to St Peter's, but it is beyond question that it was that marvellous awakener of souls, Paul, who called the humble physician of Asia Minor to Christ.

We can therefore reconstruct this evangelist's biography far more accurately than we can any of the others'. Baptized by St Paul, Luke attached himself to him. He took part in the second missionary journey (Acts 16. 10), and thereafter (except for an interruption after their stay at Philippi) followed him like his shadow, escorted him on his way to Jerusalem, and no doubt went to Caesarea when St Paul was removed there and spent two years in captivity. Intrepid in his loyalty, he did not shrink from escorting his master to Rome, sharing his famous adventures at sea in the "Castor and Pollux", serving him during his term of imprisonment in Rome, and refusing to be separated from him save by his death. Paul loved him: in the worst moment of grave danger he paid him this tribute: "Luke is my only companion" (2 Tim. 4. 11). No doubt it is he who is alluded to in 2 Corinthians (8. 18): "that brother of ours who has won the praise of all the Churches by his proclamation of the gospel". The traditional assertion, that St Luke handed on the Good News as he had heard St Paul teach it, is therefore highly probable.

Does his medical profession reveal itself in his work? In a general way, certainly, by the high intellectual qualities it reveals, but also in detail. Medical influences can, in fact, be detected in his Gospel. Luke must have closely studied the therapeutical works of his time, especially that of Dioscorides, from whom he borrowed almost word for word the first sentence of his Gospel.[10] Meticulous scholars—a thesis has been produced on it—have proved that many technical terms employed by St Luke are found in Hippocrates, Dioscorides, Galen and other Greek physicians. There are clinical indications which Luke alone seems to have known, or gives in detail: for example in the episodes of the woman with the issue of blood (8. 43), the possessed boy (9. 39) and the woman who was bent double (13. 11); only Luke records

[10] Compare the prologue of the Gospel (1. 1-4), with the following prologue of Dioscorides: "Whereas many, not only of the ancients, but of later writers, have established the relations between the preparations, the powers and the results of medicines, I shall attempt to show you, most excellent Area, that on this subject I have held an attitude neither unreasonable nor groundless."

the famous and moving detail of the sweat like blood in the Garden of Olives (22. 4). It has been pointed out, with a touch of malice, that in the story of the woman with the issue of blood, the doctor gives himself away: while Mark, with rather crude simplicity, says: "she had undergone much from many physicians, spending all she had on them, and no better for it, but rather grown worse" (5. 26), the Greek text of St Luke says more guardedly that she "had spent all her money on doctors without finding one who could cure her" (8. 43). It may then be held as beyond dispute that the third Gospel was certainly written by the Hellenist physician who was Paul's companion and disciple.[11]

It was, then, as an intelligent, well-educated man that he worked on his book. He says so himself in his prologue: before writing, he took pains to be well documented. He did not confine himself to taking down his master's words. In the Christian communities he was led to visit with St Paul he collected countless pieces of information. It was thus that he knew some of the holy women who had accompanied Christ during his mission, and he is alone in naming them with great precision (8. 2–3): among them, Joanna, the wife of Chuza, Herod's steward, no doubt informed him of what went on at the tetrarch's court.

One infinitely more precious source of information was almost certainly at his disposal: the memories of the Blessed Virgin herself. For of many facts concerning the conception, birth and childhood of Jesus, recorded in the famous first part of the Gospel, only the Mother of God could have pre-

---

[11] Some authors, however, have expressed reserved opinions on the question of Luke being a doctor. Cadbury has shown that Lucian, whom no one regards as a doctor, uses nearly all the medical terms met with in Luke. Fr Lagrange has written simply: "We are satisfied with this harmony with tradition." Canon Jacquier says: "It is difficult to give a definite opinion." The Protestant Goguel: "The conclusion of these observations is not that Luke could not have been a doctor, but simply that arguments drawn from lexicographical considerations alone cannot make it certain that he was."

served the memory. "His mother kept in her heart the memory of all this" (2. 51); all must admit that this discreet phrase from the Gospel refers to this unique informant.

Luke collected not only oral evidence: he alludes in his prologue to other works which had preceded his own. Does he mean only those memoranda which may have been used by the first catechetical teachers? It is generally agreed that he knew Matthew's Aramaic text (or rather, one of those oral translations which, as we saw, preceded the canonical Greek version), and still more probably that of Mark, for his story follows its main outlines and he has incorporated nearly the whole of its substance in his text.

He knew how to use all this documentation with intelligence and a rare sense of accuracy. He links up the events he reports with general history (3. 1–2); he tries to place words and discourses in their context (3. 15; 9. 43; 11. 1, 13; 15. 1; 18. 9), he places the Lord's Prayer, for example, at the point where Jesus taught it and not in the Sermon on the Mount. Many are the precise indications of time he provides, indicating that Christ was "about thirty years old" at the time of his mission (3. 23), noting with a word that a certain thing happened "the same day" (24. 13) or "the next day" (9. 37). A psychologist, he tried to understand the working of events: thus in four or five passages he emphasizes the hostility of the Jews against Jesus (6. 11; 11. 53; 19. 47; 20. 19).

When he wrote his Gospel, to whom did he address it? He dedicated his work to the "most noble Theophilus", that is, to an "Excellency", a person of high rank, already won over to Christian ideas. This was a custom with the ancient authors, a custom preserved in our classics, but here it has the force of a sign. Those for whom the third Gospel was destined were converted pagans, probably different from those addressed by Mark: it is known that while Peter and Paul were working together in Rome, they did not proclaim the Good News to the same circles. The text of the Gospel shows whom it had in mind. If they had been Jews, Luke would not have had to provide them with explanations which would have seemed to them quite needless, for example, to state that "the Passover is a feast of the Jews". When he gives the name of "Lake of Genesareth" to the sheet of water which the others call the "Sea of Galilee", we must see the difference of outlook as the reaction of men who knew the world better than Galilean peasants. Moreover, addressing "Gentiles", he picks out what can appeal to them, for example, the doctrine of universal salvation; but he omits what had no interest for them, such as the parallel between the Old Law and the New, or what might offend them, such as the famous saying quoted by Matthew: "My errand is only to the lost sheep which are of the house of Israel" (Matt. 15. 24).

With all this abundance of information, then, in view, we can easily see how Luke wrote his Gospel. Living with St Paul, in touch with a whole world of pagan converts attracted by the genius of the great apostle, he set himself to give them an intellectual food which should be adequate, a work "set in order", as he said himself, and sufficient not only to persuade their intelligence but to convince their hearts and confirm their faith. When did he carry out this work? Most probably when he was living in Rome, after accompanying Paul there (in 61); that is, soon after the composition of Mark's Gospel, and a little before the publication of the Greek translation of Matthew. How wonderfully fertile were those years, some thirty years after the death of Christ, when the Gospel was opening out in these three sublime flowers!

From the literary point of view, the Gospel according to St Luke is unquestionably a gem. "The loveliest book there is", says Renan. All the critics, Christian and rationalist alike, agree in admitting his incomparable gifts as an artist and a narrator. There are numerous passages of this Gospel which, like the pages of an anthology, are well known to all: the

incident of the pardon of the sinful woman, the parables of
the Good Samaritan and the Prodigal Son, the mysterious
and astounding dialogue of the risen Christ with the disciples
at Emmaus; these form part of the most genuine, the most
imperishable heritage of our civilization. What would our
feast of Christmas be if St Luke had not written his opening
"Gospel of the childhood"?

From the beginning to the end the qualities of his style are
outstanding. His Greek is not that of the great classics, but
it is correct and natural, the language spacious and flexible.
His methods are much more varied than those of the other
synoptics. When he relates the same events as Matthew and
Mark, he adds revisions of detail, always with the effect
of elegance. A certain reticence may be noticed in his narration, toning down scenes of violence—the expulsion of the
traders in the Temple, the outrages done to Jesus—and
also, though it does not lessen the fundamental tragedy, there
is a touch of tenderness and delicacy.

A rare psychologist, Luke is not content to note, like Mark,
the facial expressions and attitudes; with a word he com-
ments on them and shows the feelings behind them. So the
portraits we have in his Gospel are the most vivid, the most
clearly cut of all. Whether we think of the apostles, or Herod,
or Pilate, or even of unimportant characters like Zacchaeus
the publican, it is always through Luke's description that one
may best imagine them. One of his portraits is uniquely
valuable for us: that of our Lady, whom psychologically we
should scarcely know at all, were it not for the discreet
touches he gives us. The legendary tradition, which makes
Luke the painter of a portrait of Mary, is founded on a truth,
for at least in the literary sense of the word he is indeed
her portrait-painter.

In general, the third Gospel is constructed on a very definite
plan, in which the usual four-part plan of the synoptics is
modified by the addition of two divisions. Altogether we
find six main elements; the stories of the birth and child-

hood; Jesus' investiture in the eyes of men; his manifestation in Galilee; his preaching of salvation; his stay in Jerusalem culminating in the Passion; his Resurrection and Ascension. This plan is fairly closely followed, though some episodes, discourses or parables seem to have no absolutely determining reason for their positions. His exposition is marked by a concern for teaching, not only in general, but in particular scenes where he aims at bringing out the essentials (this is most marked in his account of the Eucharist). This mixture of didactic purpose and discreet realism results in a number of stories, well-arranged, alert and vivid. The characters are presented very accurately, often silhouetted first in a few words, then resumed and elaborated. The events are linked together with an often exquisite ease. In every way, the part which is perhaps the most skilful, and the most precious for us, is the first, where in two well-balanced cycles, that of the Annunciations and that of the Nativities, the evangelist tells us how Christ was born, with so many precise and charming details.

One observation has rightly been made about the actual manner in which he conceived the Gospel as a whole, a manner which ought to be considered in relation to the general plan of the Acts. In the Gospel, the story starts in Galilee, moves towards Jerusalem and is there fulfilled and completed. In the Acts, everything starts from Jerusalem, and widens out with the expansion of the Good News. The man who must certainly have planned the two books at the same time, and had the idea of establishing this parallelism between them, so perfectly adequate both to the profound reality and to the symbol, was without doubt a real writer.

But he is something more: a man of an exquisite conscience, a sensitive and delicate nature—"the scribe of the lovingkindness of the Lord", Dante calls him—a soul all radiant with the love of the Lord. Though influenced by the mind of St Paul, he is always simple and scarcely ventures

into those vast theological flights of the author of the great
epistles. It is not the *knowledge* of God which chiefly attracts
him, but his *love*. And to make this felt he speaks in tones
which can never be equalled; he quotes words or gives examples which never cease to console us.

This love of Christ for men, of which St Paul speaks (Tit.
3. 4), this mercy towards us sinners, has never been better
expressed than by St Luke. The parable of the Prodigal Son,
"that literary miracle of psychological power", as Mgr Ricciotti calls it, is told us by him alone. He alone shows us
the Good Shepherd going out to seek the lost sheep and
making great rejoicing when he has found it, a detail which
is lacking in St Matthew; and also the woman who seeks
and finds the lost coin, and rejoices with her friends. The
leitmotiv of St Luke is undoubtedly that lovely, consoling
verse: "There is joy among the angels of God over one sinner
that repents" (15. 8–10). And that sovereign mercy breaks
out again in the supreme moment, when Jesus in his agony
murmurs the words recorded by St Luke alone: "Father,
forgive them; they do not know what it is they are doing."

Besides this fundamental aspect of St Luke there are
others no less precious. The evangelist of love, he is also
the evangelist of purity. It is chiefly through him that we
see in Christ that delicate and chaste pity, which so utterly
contrasts with the general attitude of the ancients towards
woman. To the latent misogyny of certain parts of the Old
Testament, and to Seneca's open scorn for the *impudens
animal*, the third Gospel opposes those pure, generous sentiments expressed towards so many women, like the widow
of Naim, or Mary the sister of Martha, or the holy women
who accompanied Jesus. To that raising of woman's position
brought about by the Good News, the third Gospel has certainly been the most potent contributor.

But in this beautiful work we must not only consider the
easiest, the most indulgent aspects. It is also the Gospel of
poverty and renunciation. He who is so gentle and tender

shows himself really severe only to the Pharisees, the well-provided, the selfish, those who claim to be the just. On every occasion, it is this class of men he strikes at, through a verse of the *Magnificat* (1. 51–2), in the parable of the Prodigal Son, where the elder son is very severely judged, and on a score of like occasions. In St Matthew, the Sermon on the Mount repeats nine times the word, Blessed. In St Luke's version, the word appears only four times, but four times is heard the terrible malediction, Woe. And all four times it is to strike at the rich and those in possession. So too, while St Matthew speaks in the first Beatitude of the "poor in spirit", Luke says simply "the poor", a difference which reveals a tender predilection.

And yet, in this gospel of both penitence and mercy, the dominant impression is one of joy. The age-old slander, that because Christianity calls men to renunciation it is a religion of morose gloom, is refuted in Luke without words, simply by the deeds and words of the Lord. From the moment when the choir of angels sings in the heavens to call down on earth the lovingkindness from on high, to that moment when the return of the Holy Spirit is announced, the whole Gospel is upheld by joy and hope. It is also upheld by the highest spiritual aspiration: it is the Gospel of prayer, to which Jesus is so often seen to go apart to call on his Father; of constant, humble and earnest prayer, of prayer which still punctuates the moments of Christ's agony. Without sharing the metaphysical depths of St John, it reveals, from beginning to end, a genuinely mystical aspiration. Thus to these pagans, converts or on the road to conversion, St Luke offered just what they could best appreciate: a testimony, as overwhelming as it was vivid and accurate, to the great event for which so many of the ancients yearned in their hearts, the coming into the world of a true Saviour.

REMARKS ON THE SYNOPTICS

Anyone reading the first three gospels must be struck

by their remarkable similarity. In many passages this amounts to such a close correspondence (of which we give some examples later) that the three texts can be arranged in three parallel columns, which can be read at a glance. This *simultaneous view* or, in Greek, *synopsis*, prompted the scholar Griesbach, in 1774, to give them the name of the Synoptic Gospels. The name found general favour and has become current usage.[12]

But while the similarity is obvious, it is far from being mere copying. There are also dissimilarities, often very marked, which are not due merely to differences of the talents, style or intentions of the authors (we shall give examples of these also). It is these two facts, similarity in general, dissimilarity in detail, that create what is called the "synoptic problem", for which the exegetes have proposed so many and contradictory solutions, and this is the point to give an outline of it.

Consider first the facts. Basically, the synoptics are undoubtedly similar. Their outline is the same, very different in appearance from the fourth Gospel, since the synoptics seem to reduce Christ's public life to one year. The constituent elements of their story are largely identical: the synoptics have 350 verses in common, that is, altogether a third of St Matthew (1070 verses) and of St Luke (1151 verses) and more than half of St Mark (677 verses). Yet, as these figures indicate, there are omissions and additions as between the three. We can understand why an editor has added some information he possessed: it is less easy to see why very important facts have been neglected by one or another: why Mark, for example, should have omitted all the childhood of Jesus and the Sermon on the Mount, or why Matthew should not have recorded the Ascension. In some cases, the omission would even seem to run counter to the evident intention of the evangelist. St Luke, for

[12] There are also cases where the similarity extends to the fourth Gospel.

instance, who is writing specially for Gentiles, does not quote the touching incident of the Syrophenician woman, reported by Mark (7. 24), which would have proved that Jesus had tender feelings for the pagans who appealed to him. It is therefore impossible to deduce any general principle from these omissions and additions.

As to the succession of facts and episodes, the law of similarity applies very rarely for the three. Mark and Luke generally follow the same order (with seven exceptions), but Matthew only follows Mark's order from the fourteenth chapter. In reporting the same events, Matthew and Luke have each their own plan and method, Matthew having evidently a very keen concern for logic in his exposition. Finally, in the many passages where the general arrangement is the same, comparison of details reveals many divergences.

These differences of detail are still more striking in the matter of form. They are very numerous, and here, too, some are surprising. For example, in St Matthew and St Luke, Jesus tells his apostles, going out on their mission, to take nothing with them, "not a wallet for the journey, no second coat, no spare shoes, or *staff*", while in St Mark he tells them to take *"a staff for their journey and nothing more"*. Not a very important difference, we admit, but it proves that the evangelists have not copied one another. On the other hand, in many passages we get quite a different impression: the resemblance is such that we wonder whether they have copied or have all three used the same sources. The reader, by using the marginal references in his Bible, can compare the three texts on certain episodes; he will be impressed by the degree of these resemblances: for example, the cure of the palsied man (Matt. 9. 1–8), or the incident of the disciples plucking and eating the ears of corn (Matt. 12. 1–7), or the conversation with the rich young man (Matt. 19. 16–22). Still more striking: when the synoptics quote the Old Testament, they all do so in the same way, according to a text which is neither that of the Hebrew Bible nor that of the Greek Septuagint. The conclusion seems inevitable that because of the importance of these references they have tried to maintain a rigorous unity. But then why do they diverge over words or events which are far more important, for example, the list of the Beatitudes, the words of the Lord's Prayer, St Peter's confession, the formula of the Eucharist, the wording of the "titulus" on the cross? We can now see how complex this "synoptic problem" can be.

It must be emphasized, however, that these differences or divergences in no way detract from the superior veracity of the generally concordant testimony of the evangelists. Once we realize that the three accounts confirm one another on essentials, the dissimilarities prove that we have three testimonies blending with one another. If they flatly copied one another, nothing could prove that they spoke the truth, but because they differ, the points on which they agree have a far stronger probative value. This argument, borrowed by Fr Lagrange from the historians Langlois and Seignobos in their *Introduction aux études historiques*, must never be forgotten, for it has great weight. It is certainly one of the reasons which determined the Church, when fixing the Canon of Scripture, not to try to fuse the synoptics into one (as was done, we saw, by certain Christian writers like Tatian and the historian Eusebius), but to allow them to exist side by side.[13]

Two questions, then, immediately arise: do the synoptics depend on one another, or have they used common sources? It is even possible that the solution may be found in a third hypothesis, one which comes quite naturally to mind when one remembers the manner in which the Good News was sown in the world, that in fact the Gospel was first spoken before it was written. To be easily taught to the masses, and easily remembered by the preachers, the oral catechesis

---

[13] The other and more decisive reason being, as we have seen, respect for the venerable traditions with which the three evangelists were connected.

must have been simple and even simplified, and therefore on a purposely incomplete and schematic plan. This oral tradition must have constituted the basis of our synoptics; this must have furnished their four-part plan, their principal subjects and developments, their literary devices, with parallelisms and refrains. Papias, the Phrygian bishop who is one of the most valuable witnesses on the transmission of the Gospel, says that in the early days the "living and permanent voice" was preferred above all else: here precisely was this "living and permanent voice", this oral Gospel handed on through the exact memory of the eastern peoples and preserved in our synoptics. The differences between them are then very easily explained: the primitive catechesis varied according to the needs of the apostolate and the personalities of the apostles who handed it on. The teachings addressed to Palestinian Jews, and therefore emphasizing the Messiahship of Jesus, were not the same as those addressed to the pagans; the former would have governed the Gospel of St Matthew, the latter that of St Mark. The principle is clear, and fairly satisfying for the mind. Only "fairly", for it does not explain why certain details have remained in one or other of the texts while certain important events are neglected. At first sight, one would think that in an oral transmission the essential elements would be preserved while the details could be sacrificed. But we must remember the hypothesis pointed out in our introduction, that the preachers of the Gospel would have used little handbooks of memoranda, more or less fragmentary; it would be these written pieces which passed into the Gospels, just as they were, identical in each Gospel, but clad in the elements of the particular oral tradition.

This hypothesis has the merit of being based on what we may logically suppose to have been the historical development of the Gospel preaching. This does not mean that no other hypothesis is tenable. Some have maintained that there is formal interdependence between the evangelists, that is, that they contributed to one another. The mutual dependence of the evangelists is likewise perfectly admissible; as soon as a Gospel was written down and published abroad (like Matthew's Aramaic gospel), it is more than likely that another evangelist, before setting to work, would have consulted it. St Luke, for example, may have had in his hands, if not our present Matthew in full, at least considerable extracts; he may also have read St Mark and used it in various sections. The Greek translation of Matthew may likewise have taken account of the second Gospel. The hypothesis of mutual dependence leaves intact the problem of the differences between the three texts, and is self-explanatory, since one or other omits events which the others report. But it is partially valid and can also be reconciled with the first hypothesis: in the primitive Christian circles, the play of reciprocal actions and reactions must have been infinitely complex; they exchanged and passionately expounded the texts which some one or another had been able to write about the Saviour. To the oral tradition, to the little memoranda books, were added the first carefully edited texts: the whole must have been considered by the evangelists as materials for the great work they were carrying out.

Such, very roughly, is the hypothesis—fairly complex, we can see, as complex as life—which Catholic exegetes may hold as the most probable. "Liberal" criticism goes further and thinks it can identify some of these memoranda, these fragmentary documents used by the evangelists. German critics have maintained, with Schleiermacher, that Matthew and Luke used two sources. One, they say, was a pre-Gospel, a sort of draft, of Mark, recording actions; the other a collection of "Logia" or discourses of the Lord, a kind of catalogue of Christ's sayings, usually denoted by the letter Q (from the German *Quelle*, source). Our Gospels, then, resulted from the combination of these two elements. This is what is called the "two-sources theory". Theoretically it is not inadmissible: does not St Luke's prologue allude to earlier writings? But none of the earliest witnesses to the Gospel—such as Papias—confirms this hypothesis. Never has it been proved that there existed a collection containing only sayings of Christ, nor has the existence of "Proto-Mark" ever been demonstrated. By placing Mark first in chronological order, this theory runs counter, as we have seen, to the tradition which holds St Matthew to be the first. Moreover, how could Matthew and Luke, being so different, each depend strictly and almost exclusively on the same sources? The mistake of the two-sources theory is that it tries to explain the composition of the Gospels in an over-simple fashion, neglecting the living context in which it operated, as well as the characters of the men who composed them under the inspiration of the Holy Spirit.

We should not envisage the evangelists as scholars, writing a history-book by comparing texts, but as believers, raised above themselves by enthusiasm and faith, eager to collect all they could about the divine Master—oral traditions, written fragments, already existing texts—in order to construct from them a monument of love and truth, with the sole aim of offering, to the adoration of those whose desire is to imitate Jesus, the portrait of the One Model.[14]

THE FOURTH GOSPEL: ACCORDING TO ST JOHN

We have only to open the fourth Gospel to realize that it stands outside the tradition of the synoptics. The tone in which it is written, its plan, the author's evident intentions, are plainly different from those of Matthew, Mark and Luke. This impression is only confirmed by closer study, and it had already been observed by the Christians of the earliest centuries. John supplies many pieces of information unknown

[14] Examples of parallel narratives in the Synoptic Gospels and of a quadruple synopsis (the first multiplication of the loaves) can be found, printed in parallel columns, in *What is the Bible?* by Daniel-Rops, in this series, pp. 118–125.

to the synoptics. Eusebius of Caesarea, who divided the
Gospels into sections for purposes of comparison, notes that
out of 232 sections, John has 106 which owe nothing to
the others. Anyone who reads the celebrated Johannine prologue: "In the beginning was the Word..." can measure
the gulf between the inspired poet who wrote those lines
and the other evangelists.

The difference between the synoptics and the fourth Gospel
is therefore twofold: a difference of documentation and a
difference of accent. The things John says are not the same
as those said by his predecessors, and he does not say them
with the same purpose. It may be well to note that these
differences in no way affect the profound identity of the
message conveyed by the four texts. But they are nonetheless revealing of the man who wrote the book and of the
conditions in which he wrote.

One first observation must be made: since the author fails
to repeat a great part of what the synoptics had said, but
instead adds personal information, it must be admitted that
he was almost certainly addressing Christians who were
familiar with the contents of the synoptics, but thought it
infinitely desirable to possess supplementary information on
the subject nearest their hearts. In the abstract, then, we
may suppose the author to have been a witness with private
sources of information, who had studied the synoptics and
designed, with full knowledge of the subject, to supplement
them. We may qualify this by saying that this Gospel gives
the impression of intending not only to perfect the earlier
ones but to throw a clearer light on the actions and message
of Christ. Several times it lays stress on the fact that the
apostles themselves did not, at the time, understand their
Master's intentions. It was only later, through meditation,
that the author had really penetrated them; which leads
to the conclusion that between the events and the writing
of them in the Gospel a somewhat long period had elapsed.

Equally significant conclusions follow from another observation, concerning the relations between the author and

Israel, which are complex and apparently almost contradictory. On the one hand he denounces the rebellious people,
which has refused to recognize the Messiah and is doomed
to all catastrophes: in his condemnation he is even stricter
than St Paul, who accompanies his condemnation with an
infinite hope. On the other hand, even as a Christian, he
is still faithful to the message handed down by Israel, that
people from whom "salvation is to come"; who worship,
"knowing what it is we worship"; the people which has
been the Lord's spokesman, the chosen scribe, the trustee
of Scripture, "whose words have binding force". At the
same time, there can be no doubt that the author is of
Jewish origin. This is proved by his style, full of Semitisms
in form and vocabulary, constructed on those parallelisms
so characteristic of the Hebrew sentence. He quotes and
translates Hebrew or Aramaic terms, such as Rabbi, Messiah,
Cephas, Siloë, Rabboni. He speaks accurately of the Jewish
customs concerning feasts, rites and legal prescriptions, while
the way in which he explains them proves that he was not
addressing Israelites. Finally, the author gives the impression
of knowing Palestine at first-hand, Galilee as well as Jerusalem—a striking fact which did not escape the notice of
Renan, as we shall see later. He was certainly, then, a Jew,
who must have been with Jesus on his mission, who was
keenly conscious of the gratitude a Christian ought to feel
towards the people of the Old Law, but had also sorrowfully
measured the abyss which henceforth yawned between Jews
of the Torah and Jews of the Gospel.

His book seems to be stamped with another intention,
namely, to rectify certain doctrinal errors in the heart of
Christianity. We know from the history of the Church that
heresies arose by the end of the first century, and this may
be considered in relation to an assertion of St Irenaeus, that
the fourth Gospel was aimed at Cerinthus, a heretic who
maintained that the Christ-God had descended on the man
Jesus at his baptism, under the form of the Dove, but had

abandoned him at the time of the Passion. In the first Epistle, which is by the same author as the Gospel, this intention of refutation is obvious: it also seems to be implied in the gospel, which leads us to the conclusion that this was composed at a time and in a spiritual climate in which the danger of theological discussions had already been revealed.

In conclusion, a purely literary point may be noticed. The fourth Gospel, from this point of view, is far from equalling the third; its language is often awkward, its vocabulary rather limited. If it is so moving, it is because of qualities which surpass those of the stylist. We have noted its Semitic manner: this is so marked that an earlier Aramaic version has been suggested, as for Matthew, and this hypothesis has been abandoned only because tradition does not provide a single argument in its support. We have then a clear impresssion of a Jew writing in Greek, in a generally correct manner, but without real vigour or ease, and without being really transformed by Greek culture.

Such are the main conclusions reached by "internal criticism" of the fourth Gospel: it is striking to note that they all wonderfully coincide with the Church's traditional assertion, that the author of this fourth Gospel is St John the Apostle.

None of the synoptic Gospels expressly names its author. In the fourth, however, is found a formal though mysterious indication. The text is practically concluded with the statement: "It is the same disciple that bears witness of all this and has written the story of it" (21. 24), "the same" referring to "the disciple whom Jesus loved", mentioned in v. 20. The question therefore comes down to this: who was the disciple whom Jesus loved? He is mentioned several times in the course of the Gospel, for the first time in 13. 23. Before that he is not named, but we see a disciple who certainly seems to be the same, a disciple who is among the first to follow Jesus, who offers himself with Andrew, brother of Simon Peter; he certainly seems to be John. Similarly, during the Passion, the unnamed disciple who was "the high priest's acquaintance", and brought Peter into the court of the high priest's palace, appears again to be John. If we go by the witness of the synoptics, this disciple, honoured by Jesus with a special friendship, cannot be sought beyond the circle of the three who were visibly favoured: Peter, James the Greater and John. But as Peter assumes quite a different rôle in the Gospel, as James was martyred in 44, that is, certainly before the writing of this Gospel, the conclusion is that the author was John. To this we may add that the care on the author's part never to name John or his brother James, or Zebedee their father, or that Salome who was most probably "the mother of Zebedee's sons" and whose presence was noted by Matthew and Mark at Calvary and at the tomb, has also the value of a sign: it was from humility that John refrained from writing these names.

This attribution is confirmed in the most categorical fashion by tradition, and we may add that the most recent discoveries, such as the second-century papyri in Egypt, have not ceased to support it. And another point must be noted: the fourth Gospel, precisely because it is very different from the synoptics, must be authentic, if we remember the care of the primitive Church to banish all doctrinal deviation, to reject apocryphal documents, and certainly it would have taken nothing less than the authority of one of the first apostles to ensure its acceptance. Now, this Gospel was used by the Church from the beginning of the second century, in the letters of St Ignatius of Antioch, in the "Odes of Solomon", in the Apologies of St Justin (about 135), and even in heretical Montanist and Gnostic texts. At the end of the century, there are numerous explicit testimonies attributing the fourth Gospel to St John. The Muratorian Canon defends its Johannine authorship, St Irenaeus quotes this attribution as something self-evident, and his testimony is of special importance because, being a native of Asia Minor and a disciple of St Polycarp, he is directly linked with those who had known John.

He writes: "John, the Lord's disciple, who had leaned on his breast, he too gave forth his gospel, while he was dwelling in Ephesus." Still more explicit is a sentence of Clement of Alexandria, quoted by the historian Eusebius: "Seeing that the gospels had set forth only the material story, John, the last of them all, entreated by his disciples, and upheld by the Spirit, wrote the spiritual gospel."[15]

Thus the twofold testimony of the Gospel itself and of tradition affirms that its author was John. It so happens that he is one of the apostles whose life and personality can be most easily reconstructed from the New Testament. A young Jew (his name means "Yahweh gives grace"), a Galilean, brother of James the Greater, son of Zebedee and Salome, in Christ's lifetime he must have been a very young man, almost an adolescent, which would explain the tenderness, as of an elder brother, shown him by Jesus. From the moment when, with Andrew, he gave himself to Christ, we get the impression that he never left him. He is one of the three witnesses of the raising of Jairus' daughter, of the Transfiguration, of the Agony. With Peter he was given the task of preparing the Last Supper. At the foot of the cross he stood by Mary, and it was to him that Jesus entrusted her. The mutual confidence between him and Jesus was such that, in order to ask questions of Christ, the other disciples had recourse to him, as is seen at the Last Supper. A loving, generous and passionate nature—"Son of Thunder", as Jesus affectionately called him (Mark 3. 17)—a fiery soul who desired the first place in the kingdom, but also said he was ready to drink the Lord's cup; let us add, a conscience of crystal purity and, if we may trust those mirrors of tradition, Tertullian and St Jerome, of perfect virginity.

[15] Others translate: "the gospel of spiritual aspects".

In what conditions did John write his Gospel? We may guess them by following the course of his life after Pentecost. Companion of Peter in the first days of the apostolate, present at the Council of Jerusalem in 49 which decided the Church's attitude to the converts from paganism, he is lost sight of for some time, but when Jerusalem falls to the siege of the Romans in 70, he is to be found in Asia, at Ephesus, where he took St Paul's place and carried on his work. This residence in Ephesus is assured by all tradition, notably by Tertullian, Clement of Alexandria, Irenaeus and even the apocryphal gospels. According to Tertullian, he underwent at Rome, under Domitian in 95 or 96, the torture of boiling oil, from which he emerged unhurt (a detail which is not an article of faith), and was then banished to the island of Patmos. Freed under Nerva, he is said to have returned to Ephesus, where he spent the last years of his life and died at an advanced age under Trajan.[16] Ephesus boasted of preserving his tomb.

The Gospel is certainly later than 70, for it presumes it to be known that Peter has been martyred, that everything in Jerusalem has been overwhelmed in catastrophe, that the condemnation of the Jews and the call of the Gentiles were admitted facts. Constant tradition affirms that the fourth Gospel was preceded by the writing of another great Johannine work, the Apocalypse, composed about 95–6. On the other hand, since the influence of John can be seen, as we saw, on texts of the early second century, like St Ignatius' letters and the so-called Odes of Solomon, we must conclude that the only period in which the Gospel could have been written is between 96 and 100. We may then suppose events to have been as follows: John returned to Ephesus as a venerated nonagenarian, crowned with the glory of martyrdom. During his long life he had deeply pondered the un-

[16] Trajan reigned from 98 to 117. It is scarcely credible that, if John was a young man in 30, he could have long survived the year 100.

forgettable experiences of his youth. He had read the other
Gospels, he had deepened his understanding of the divine
message. His words, when he taught the Church at Ephesus,
were so beautiful, so fresh and yet so right, that his hearers
begged him to put his teaching into writing. He did so, and
thus appeared this supreme document.

This interpretation of the facts, which is highly probable,
also enables us to reply to an objection: how could the
text of the fourth Gospel, so profound, so full of sweeping
metaphysical flights, have been the work of a former fisherman on the Lake of Galilee? To this it may be replied,
first, that John, as the son of an obviously well-to-do fishing
manager, could well have been educated and moreover most
of Israel's great rabbis earned their living by manual labour.
But above all, if it is true that between the death of Christ
and the writing of this Gospel seventy years had elapsed,
there might well be a gulf between the youth of the thirties
and the old man at the end of the century. John had all
this time in which to perfect his education, to develop his
speculative gifts, especially in those Hellenized circles of
Asia Minor where the interplay of ideas was carried to a
high degree of perfection. What the young fisherman of Bethsaida could not do was well within the capacity of the
hoary sage of Ephesus.[17]

[17] On this question of the authorship of the fourth Gospel, we
may here note some difficulties. The first is the undoubted difference
of language between the Apocalypse and the Gospel, though this
is not so great as some have said, for many of their words, images
and constructions are identical. It is granted, however, that for the
Gospel, the language of which is more finished, the apostle might
have had recourse to a secretary, which would not have been possible
during his exile in Patmos. The second concerns three passages
which some have denied to be by John. One is the incident of the
angel at the pool (5. 3, 4), which may reflect a popular tradition.
The second is the celebrated story of the woman taken in adultery
(7. 53–8. 11), which is certainly canonical, but its style is rather
synoptic than Johannine, and it may have been inserted by a copyist.
The third is the conclusion (21. 24), in which some wrongly see
an unnecessary repetition, also due to a copyist.

From what we have now seen of the conditions in which the fourth Gospel was written, it is easy to understand the two poles of interest it contains: on the one hand it provides fresh documents on our knowledge of Christ, on the other it offers an interpretation of his rôle and message directly linked with that which Christ himself must have held.

The contribution of the fourth Gospel to our documentation about Christ is extremely important. Contrary to the opinions of a whole tribe of rationalist critics, led by Loisy, that the fourth Gospel is "a theological theorem which has great difficulty in preserving the appearance of history", the most searching study, the most recent archaeological discoveries, prove that John is an exact and scrupulously precise source of information. Renan, the first historian to attempt to rediscover Jesus in his time and setting, does not hesitate to write: "The historical sketch of the fourth Gospel is, in my view, the life of Jesus as it was known in the immediate entourage of John.... I must admit that in my opinion this school was better acquainted with various circumstances of the life of the Founder than the group whose remembrances constituted the synoptic Gospels."

On the order of events and of history, the fourth Gospel undoubtedly adds to the synoptics. He supplements, he rectifies, he qualifies. For example, he emphasizes the ministry in Judaea, about which the others, absorbed in the events in Galilee, have little to say. He tells us that Jesus came five times to Jerusalem, while the others seem to blend the five visits into one. While the subject-matter of the synoptics might be comprised in a single year, that of the fourth Gospel cannot be thus confined, and we understand—what is much more likely—that Christ's mission lasted two or three years.

This allegedly metaphysical editor is the one who provides the most detailed geographical information. Clearly he is remarkably familiar with Palestine. He pin-points Cana, Bethsaida, Capharnaum, Sichar, the two Bethanies, as well as

the sites and buildings of Jerusalem. He describes the holy
City as it was in our Lord's lifetime, not as it was when his
story was written, a time when it lay in utter ruins. Some
of his details, which seem surprising, have been fully confirmed by archaeological excavations: such are the "pool
with five porches" mentioned in 5. 2, and, very probably,
the "pavement" (*Lithostrotos*) to which John refers in connection with Jesus' appearance before Pilate (19. 13).

St John's story is framed in a precise chronology: he mentions the Jewish feasts which mark out the year; he clearly
indicates the Lord's comings and goings; he lets us feel time
and distance. He shows us the gradual development of
Christ's message in a way which is almost musical, by the
repetition and development of a theme.

As for the points of detail he supplies, they are countless.
The synoptics, for example, do not tell us who the brave
disciple was, who unsheathed his sword when Christ was
arrested and cut off the guard's ear: St John knew that it
was Peter, and the wounded man's name was Malchus. The
fourth Gospel says that when Jesus was arrested he was
first taken before the former high priest Annas, before being
taken to Caiaphas, and he explains why: because of the
influence this man still retained. When Peter is about to
penetrate into the high priest's court, John shows him waiting a moment before the gate, while another disciple (doubtless John himself) goes to speak for him. Again, John alone
records the memorable and dramatic moment of the *Ecce
Homo*. Examples could be multiplied.

To sum up, then, in the precise terms of the Biblical Commission (decree of May 29th, 1907), "in spite of the unique
character of the fourth Gospel, and the author's manifest
intention to prove and defend the divinity of Jesus Christ,
we must not depart from the constant practice of the Church,
which has always relied on this gospel as a genuinely historical
document". Whence did John derive this document? Quite
simply, from his own recollections, most probably preserved

in his memory, perhaps helped out by some memoranda, like those used by the first preachers of the Gospel. The differences between his text and that of the synoptics, which rationalist critics have been pleased to exaggerate and emphasize, are in fact perfectly explicable, if we remember that John knew the synoptics at the time when he wrote, and consequently could judge it more useful to supplement them than to repeat them. One of the most striking examples of this intention is to do with the Eucharist. St John does not relate the story of it, but he has perfectly explained its meaning in advance, in his famous discourse on the Bread of Life. But it is absolutely untrue to say that the Christ of the synoptics and the Christ of the fourth Gospel are different. The Jesus of St John is no less sensitive and tender than the Jesus of St Luke, no less near to us and our nature than the Jesus of St Mark. Only, in his long meditation, in the experience he had gained of the prodigious expansion of Christianity, in the knowledge he had acquired of the fulfilment of Christ's promises, John had come to understand, more fully than the others, the complete equality of the Son with the Father; it is this divine radiance of the Master which he tried, in the evening of his life, to express in his text, and that is its supreme merit.

In the spiritual order, it is certainly the fourth Gospel which leads us highest. It is indeed "the Gospel of spiritual aspects". But at the same time we must note that its lofty speculations never assume the schematic and desiccated aspect we find in metaphysical treatises. We feel that they spring from an intimate experience, they presume a commitment of the whole being. And that, moreover, is what makes the grandeur and beauty of this text, written without premeditated art, without literary pretensions, almost negligently. The author excels in communicating to us what he himself has experienced in contact with the divine Model. Fr Lagrange has well said that some of St John's phrases are really breathtaking, and he quotes, as examples of those staggering phrases, the evangelist's note, when Judas plunged into the darkness of his crime: "It was night"; and Mary Magdalene, realizing she is addressed by the Risen Christ, and murmuring the one word: "Master!" In no other Gospel does one grasp in such a penetrating manner that the one and only salvation is in Christ and the sole irremediable evil is to refuse oneself to him.

Thus the intention always implied in the fourth Gospel (and expressly stated in 20. 31) is perfectly clear: John wishes to prove that Jesus is the Messiah, the Son of God. By means of the story of the life of Christ, it is faith in Christ that he would arouse in his hearers' souls, so that, following him, they may have eternal life. It is therefore essentially an *apologia*, a theological Gospel.

The Messianic dignity of Jesus is very clearly revealed in it. The fulfilment of the prophecies in Christ is repeatedly emphasized. On many occasions, and more definitely than in the synoptics, Christ declares himself to be the Son of God, the one sent by the Father. He says that his deeds and works constitute the proof of his mission. He affirms that he existed before his coming into the world. All this lofty image culminates in that celebrated prologue in which Christ is presented as the Word of God; a prologue so beautiful, so inspired with faith and hope that Columbus, it is said, in the blackest hours of his great maritime adventure, used to repeat it to himself, in the prow of his caravel.

The Son of God is light and truth. These two words recur many times in the Gospel. Jesus says it himself: he is the light which enlightens men and gives them life: he is the truth which makes them free. Through the length of the fourth Gospel, then, there resounds an immense appeal to faith: whoever does not believe in Jesus is his own judge and will die in his sins; but whoever believes in him receives the divine life which is life eternal. More than light, more even than truth, Jesus is life. "I am the way, the truth and the life", and this gift of life which he bestows is the result of

God's love. God has loved men; he has loved them by sending his Son. Thus all that pertains to the order of salvation proceeds from this love. In the last resort, then, it is to this love that man must respond, by reflecting it in some way, by echoing it. Love is, then, the object of the new commandment (13. 34); joining hands with St Paul, whose work he had taken over in Asia Minor, the fourth evangelist profoundly convinces us that the only path to the highest spiritual realities is the path of charity.

Two special aspects of the Johannine message must be underlined. One is his symbolism. It is absolutely certain that many of the perfectly factual incidents recorded in the Gospel have a particular resonance, which enriches them with a spiritual significance. Incidents like the multiplication of the loaves, the cure of the man born blind, or the washing of the feet on Maundy Thursday evening, are described with a marked *arrière-pensée*: they are signs. Symbolism, which existed already, but much less clearly, in the synoptics, gives this Gospel a peculiar sonority, which makes it, in a literary sense, a work of the sublimest poetry. Beneath the words, one feels the thrill of an ineffable reality: there is hardly a passage in St John which cannot be expounded on two and sometimes three levels: the level of the historical record of a fact; that of its relations with the Old Testament and the prophecies; that of the future of the world. Thus the Temple which must be destroyed and rebuilt is at once the Temple in Jerusalem, doomed to destruction in history, the body of Christ himself, destined to die and rise again, and the Church, the new Temple of redeemed mankind. This ever-present symbolism, colouring the evangelist's style and making it shine with the brilliance of its antitheses and the play of its allusions, is certainly one of the characters which make it the most attractive.

In no passage does this appear with more striking effect than in the famous prologue: "In the beginning was the Word...." Here, in these affirmations of exceptional poetic beauty, is found the union of an historical statement and a

theological vision. For John, doubt is impossible: Jesus is
indeed the Word of God, and of this Word of God John
has indeed "had sight of his glory, glory such as belongs
to the Father's only-begotten Son," John adopts this term
"Word", *Logos*, rethinks it, gives it a totally new sense.
The Logos is no longer the abstract law governing the universe,
as in Heraclitus, nor the vital force animating creation, as
in the Stoics, nor even that archetype of the world and that
agent by whom God brought it into being, as the Neoplatonists
held. It surpasses even the Logos of Philo, the Jewish thinker
of Alexandria, who made it the pattern of the visible world,
an imperfect representation of God, the intermediary halfway
between the Almighty and the created world. It was not
from these various systems that John derived his affirmation,
but from actual meditation on the Christian revelation, in
the light of the Spirit. To him, the Word is God, identical
with the Father, perfect and sovereign revealer, expression
of the eternal Wisdom, in whom are fulfilled all the truths
partially conceived by the Greek philosophers, and at the
same time all those elaborated in the Old Testament. To
recognize in Jesus the living incarnation of the Word—that
was the most incontestable mark of genius of the fourth
Gospel, that in which the imprint of the Holy Spirit is most
clear. As God's Thought, the Word enlightens men; as God's
Word, he calls them; as God's Life, he is their life. Here
we can see how far the Christian revelation surpasses ancient
thought, by embracing all its valid elements and raising them
to another plane.

We cannot better conclude than by quoting the admirable
words with which Origen, the great Alexandrian thinker of
the third century, concludes his meditations on St John:
"We dare to proclaim that the gospels are the flower of
all the Scriptures, but the flower of all the Gospels is the
Gospel delivered by John, and no one can perceive its meaning who has not rested on the heart of Jesus, or to whom
Jesus has not given Mary to be his mother."

NOTE ON THE TRANSMISSION OF THE TEXT OF THE GOSPELS

by François Amiot, P.S.S.

The original text of the Gospels, as of the other New Testament scriptures, was probably written on rolls of papyrus, too fragile to stand prolonged use, and therefore bound to disappear before long. Of these we possess only manuscript copies: fragments on papyrus, some of which date from the second century; parchments containing the complete text, the oldest of which are of the fourth century. The time-interval between these manuscripts and the originals is far less than it is for profane authors, for most of whom we possess no manuscripts earlier than the ninth century, leaving a gap of from twelve to fourteen centuries between the copies and the originals.

The Gospel is no less favoured in the number of its manuscripts: more than 4,000 Greek manuscripts, including about 50 papyri of 170 uncial (that is, majuscule) manuscripts, all earlier than the ninth century, and 1,500 lectionaries, later than the seventh century.

Among the papyri the following should be noted:

The Chester Beatty papyri (third century and late second century) discovered in Egypt since 1930; these are codices, that is, in book form, not scrolls; they include fragments of the four Gospels and a large part of St Paul and the Apocalypse;

the Egerton papyri (third and late second centuries),

discovered in Middle Egypt in 1934; they comprise six fragments concerning the Jews' hostility to Christ; they borrow from the Gospels, especially from St John, and partly from oral tradition;

the John Rylands papyrus, discovered in 1920 and published in 1935; particularly precious, for it dates from about 130 and contains a fragment of St John (18. 31–3 and 37–8);

the Bodmer papyri, discovered in 1956, giving the whole of St John and large parts of St Luke.

Among the uncial manuscripts which are the oldest and the most important for the reconstruction of the text may be mentioned:

the *Vaticanus*, of the mid-fourth century, but probably reproducing a second-century text; in the Vatican Library;

the *Sinaiticus*, of the fourth century; discovered by the German Tischendorf at St Catherine's Monastery on Mount Sinai, in 1844 and 1859; in the British Museum;

the *Alexandrinus*, of the fifth century; in the British Museum;

the *Codex Aephremi rescriptus*; fifth century; a palimpsest, on which some treatises of St Ephrem were written over the text of the New Testament, in the thirteenth century; in the *Bibliothèque Nationale*, Paris;

the *Codex Bezae*, or *Cantabrigiensis*; sixth century, once belonged to the Protestant theologian Beza; Greek and Latin manuscript; in the Cambridge University Library.

Among all the manuscripts, the quotations from the Fathers earlier than the seventh century, and the ancient versions (which being literal translations enable us to recover the original text), we can find about 250,000 variants. The majority are insignificant, concerning only the spelling and order of words. According to Hort, seven-eighths of the text is undisputed; variants which affect the meaning concern only a thousandth part of the text. Only about fifty have any importance, while none affects the substance of dogma, which is sufficiently established by the critically certain passages, without having recourse to doubtful texts.

The variants are due to many causes:

The large numbers of copies, dating from different periods;

errors due to the eye, producing confusions between letters, omissions when two phrases end with the same word, faulty divisions of words, for in the early centuries these were not separated;

errors of hearing in cases of dictation: the scribe has confused the vowels or diphthongs of his original;

errors of memory in quotations from the Old Testament; sometimes, the introduction into one Gospel of a parallel passage taken from another;

intentional variants, more difficult to detect; due to falsifications by certain heretics, to the desire to improve a corrupt text or to avoid the appearance of contradiction between the Gospels: terms replaced by their synonyms; introduction of marginal glosses into the text, etc.

The existence of the variants raises the difficult problem of the *reconstruction of the text*, which is the ultimate aim of textual criticism. To this end, one tries to determine which are the oldest texts and to group the documents by families, working on the presence of identical variants, which denote a common origin. This is a very difficult task, which has occasioned immense labours, ever since the Renaissance.

A great many scholars, following Fr Lagrange in his monumental work, *Critique textuelle* (*Études Bibliques*, *Gabalda*), now consider that we can distinguish four principal recensions, that is, four states of the text:

Recension D: the oldest, represented by the *Codex Bezae*, the papyri, the old Latin versions, the Syriac versions (including the *Diatessaron* of Tatian); it is a harmonizing and popular recension, emanating from Alexandria, but widely diffused in the West, whence its long-accustomed name of the Western text. It contains numerous variants, some of which are worth retaining. It was early supplanted by other recensions and by the Latin Vulgate of St Jerome;

Recension B: which some consider the best, represented chiefly by the *Vaticanus*, the *Sinaiticus*, partially by the *Aephremi rescriptus*; it is also found in the papyri, in many uncial and minuscule manuscripts, and in Clement of Alexandria, Origen and St Athanasius. This recension has been established critically and on good manuscripts, but it must not be accorded absolute authority;

Recension A: the most elegant, represented by the *Alexandrinus*, some uncials, then by the mass of the manuscripts, especially the minuscules, the Syriac Peshitta and finally by all the Fathers from the fourth century, particularly St John Chrysostom. It is the text called the ecclesiastical or Byzantine, adopted by the scholars of the Renaissance period under the name of the Received Text. A compromise between B and D, it sacrifices too much to harmonization and elegance. It originated from Antioch or perhaps Alexandria; its official adoption at Constantinople caused it to influence a large number of manuscripts;

Recension C: revealed by recent discoveries and often called the Caesarean. It is represented by the Chester Beatty papyri, the Freer and Koridethi manuscripts, the Ferrar group, the Armenian and Georgian versions, Origen (in part) and Eusebius. It is an attempt which is earlier than A, and of the same type, but it has perished. Fr Lagrange believes that it came from Alexandria, whence it went to Caesarèa and Jerusalem. The text is fully established only for Mark.

Once the manuscript families and the value of the recensions have been established, it remains to decide between the divergent authorities for the final establishment of the text. This is a very delicate task, the results of which must remain to some extent hypothetical. To accomplish it, one must rely on the rules of what is called rational criticism, which we summarize as follows:

1. The reading more difficult to understand must be

preferred to the easier, unless it is quite unreasonable; copyists have in general a tendency to eliminate obscure or less fluent readings.

2. The shorter reading must be preferred to the longer, unless it is totally absent from the ancient manuscripts, or evades a difficulty.

3. The reading which seems to be the source of others is to be preferred; corrections which seem intentional are to be rejected; a very difficult principle to apply.

4. Preference is given to readings most in conformity with the language of the New Testament, with the author's style, manner of thought, etc., which often leads to the admission of readings bearing the mark of the Semitic mind, rather than more elegant readings.

Each of these principles has to be checked by the others, as each is open to objections. In one sense, New Testament criticism is still in the stage of experiment. In other respects, however, we may say with Fr Lagrange that the New Testament writings, in their substance, have come down to us in a state of integrity which is truly marvellous.

(Consult: Daniel-Rops, *Jesus in his Time*, Introduction; the *New Testament*; *St John*; Vaganay, *Introduction to the textual criticism of the New Testament*.)

CHAPTER V

THE GOSPEL BEFORE THE GOSPELS

by Amédée Brunot, S.C.J.

What historical knowledge of Jesus can we gain from the Acts of the Apostles and the Epistles, especially those of St Paul? For anyone trying to collect the sources of the story of Christ, the answer to this question is at first sight disappointing, for these documents tell us nothing we do not already know from the Gospels.

Closer research, however, leads to an illuminating discovery. We begin by remarking that the information provided by the Acts and the Epistles, brief as it is, confirms the facts given in the Gospels. This is all the more interesting in that the sources, originating from different surroundings, are independent of one another.

But there is more to it than that. Our synoptic Gospels, in their present text, date from more than thirty years after the events they record. Before being consigned to writing they underwent a gradual elaboration, and to detect and define this work of stratification is the chosen task of the critical school called "the method of the history of literary forms", or "Form Criticism". The deeds and words of Jesus were first entrusted to the faith of the apostles; they handed them on orally to the Churches; these in their turn constructed short literary units to which they gave a liturgical or theological polish; then followed the first essays at compilation; finally the evangelists collected these works and stamped them with their own personal imprint.

Now with the Acts and St Paul's Epistles we draw nearer to the primary sources. We are in contact with the documents almost in their pure state, echoes of the very earliest catechesis. We are almost touching Jesus himself. Further, we listen to the first orchestration of the Master's teaching and actions, we hear the first reverberation of that life in the life of the young Churches. It is truly the Gospel before the Gospels.

THE ACTS OF THE APOSTLES

But is it not an untruth to claim that the Acts of the Apostles preceded the Gospels? Is not the "second treatise" of Luke the chronological sequel of the first? Its date of composition is much later than that of the third Gospel.

True: but we know too that Luke, as conscientious an historian as he was a polished man of letters, sought out his documents with care. His sources are numerous and of very diverse origins; some are very ancient, even primitive, coming from the first communities of Jerusalem, Caesarea and Antioch.

Now this very archaic character of his information is one of the major points of interest about the Acts. In order to give us a picture of the initial catechesis, that of the very morning of Pentecost and the months following it, Luke has inserted in the early part of his work six discourses which are Jewish in tone from beginning to end.

1. St Peter's discourse to the Jews of Jerusalem after the descent of the Spirit, on the morning of Pentecost (2. 22–36).

2. The instruction given by Peter in the Temple, after the miracle at the Beautiful Gate (3. 16–26).

3. The first apostolic profession of faith before the Sanhedrin (4. 8–12).

4. The second profession of faith (5. 29–32).

5. Peter's discourses at the baptism of the centurion Cornelius (10. 34–43).

6. St Paul's discourse at Antioch in Pisidia before an audience of Jews and pagans (13. 25–41).

They are passages of unique interest. Certainly, they are only *summaries* of the apostolic preaching in the very earliest days of the Church, and they are coloured with the language and ideas of St Luke. All the same, there is nothing artificial about these summaries. The critical school we have mentioned does not hesitate to conclude that they reproduce instructions actually delivered by the apostles in definite circumstances and before actual audiences. They are truly authentic traces of that catechesis which, as the Epistles reveal, was so important in those first days of the Church.

Experts can recognize elements which are racy of the soil of Judaea. In any case, it can easily be tested: a phrase like that used by Peter, to insist that it was really Jesus who had cured the lame man, is revealing: "Here is a man you all know by sight, who has put his faith in that name, and that name has brought him strength." Here is the very Aramaic which Peter spoke by the lakeside (Acts 3. 16). We have here the most archaic documents in the New Testament.

We may go further. "The Christology expressed in it seems so primitive that there could be nothing more ancient" (Schmitt). We can overhear on the disciples' lips the first titles they gave to "Jesus of Nazareth": he is the "servant" of God (3. 13, Westminster), the "Just" and the "holy one" (3. 14), the "author" and "prince" of life (3. 15; 5. 31). They speak of the Master with all the simplicity and familiarity of the early days. The prestige of the unknown does not yet operate, as it would on those who had not known those days of intimacy. We rejoice to hear the accents of those who have heard him and seen him and remember the nostalgia of his parting. What a unique moment in the history of the Church!

How simple it all is! In the days of his earthly life "Jesus of Nazareth"—still the everyday title—was simply "a man duly accredited to you from God; such were the miracles and signs which God did through him in your midst, as you yourselves well know" (2. 22). Where would have been the good of insisting on telling the story of that life to men who had witnessed it and benefited from it?

There is rather more insistence on the Passion, for Peter, who is trying to convert his hearers, wants to face them with their grave responsibilities. So we have some precious details: "You gave him up, and disowned him in the presence of Pilate, when Pilate's voice was for setting him free" (3. 13). "You disowned the holy, the just, and asked for the pardon of a murderer, while you killed the author of life" (3. 14). "Jesus, the man you hung on a gibbet to die" (5. 30). "The people at Jerusalem, like their rulers, did not recognize Jesus for what he was; unwittingly they fulfilled, by condemning him, those utterances of the prophets which they had heard read, sabbath after sabbath. And although they could find no capital charge against him, they petitioned Pilate for his death. So, when they had fulfilled all that had been written about him, they took him down from the cross and laid him in a tomb" (13. 27–9).

Now this Jesus, thus done to death, is alive: he is risen. For the chosen people first of all, he has become "the Saviour Christ". With this title of "Lord and Christ" (2. 36), he has been "received" (3. 21) into heaven, until the day when he will again be sent to earth to inaugurate the last age, conceived in the purest biblical tradition as "the time when all is restored anew" (3. 20–1).

Reading this primitive proclamation, we realize all that the Acts add to the Gospel story of Jesus. With the synoptics, we have the impression that the event of Easter is no more than the simple conclusion of the Gospel revelation. We observe that Matthew and Mark scarcely stress the primary importance of the Resurrection. But, thanks to these fragments of the earliest catechesis, two facts of decisive importance are brought into prominence: the Paschal faith was the nucleus round which the whole Creed of the infant Church was organized, and Christ, risen alive from the tomb, often seen by his disciples and established as Lord of all, was the heart of the apostles' preaching, long before the composition of the Gospels.

We have not come to the end of our discoveries. We know that some critics have said that the "heavenly Jesus" is the fruit of the belief of the primitive community. There is, they say, a gulf between the Jesus of history and the Jesus of faith. These vestiges of the apostolic catechesis guarantee the meeting-point of faith and history. History and faith form a unity; they meet in a person, and in a definition of the person: Jesus the Christ.

These discourses from the Acts testify that the first proclamation of the risen Jesus is rooted in the earthly, Galilean reality of the Son of Mary, of the house of David. Our first preachers did not treat Jesus as a myth, and everything shows that nothing was further from their minds than to substitute a heavenly being for the Jesus of history. The event of Easter cannot possibly be explained if it is separated from the humbled life of Jesus. "Thus the faith is neither a spontaneous creation nor a satellite without a launching-pad" (B. Rigaux).

By thus firmly underlining that the centre of the primitive catechesis is neither a philosophy nor an ethic, nor even a preaching, but the person of Jesus of Nazareth, the Acts demonstrate that there is continuity between the earthly and the glorified Jesus. The faith of the Jerusalem community is essentially historic. The link with the human life of Jesus is such that the Church is careful to keep witnesses from among "men who have walked in our company all through the time when the Lord Jesus came and went among us, from the time when John used to baptize till the day when he, Jesus, was taken from us" (1. 21–2). This earthly life is guaranteed by the community: "God has raised up this man Jesus from the dead; we are all witnesses of it" (2. 32; cf. 3. 15; 4. 35; 5. 32). And this community is no nameless mob, but a group under a hierarchy, inspired and guided by official witnesses. Tradition and authority: these are its marks. Further, their zeal in unmasking the *fables* testifies to a desire for truth about the past.

To these first witnesses, the Resurrection is as historical as the baptism or the death on the cross. How all the testimonies insist on the bodily character of the glorified Christ! Jesus, though dead and buried, "did not see corruption" (2. 31). From the outset they based their conviction on the reality of the empty tomb: on the very morning of Pentecost Peter contrasted the Resurrection of Jesus with the fate of "the patriarch David", who "did die and was buried, and his tomb is among us to this day" (2. 29). The empty tomb of Christ is an historical fact: Jews and disciples alike know it well.

As to the appearances, the apostles lay most stress on their evidence to the senses. They were marked by many actions, they were repeated "over a space of many days" (13. 31), and were represented as a continued contact of Christ with his own, a contact similar to that common life which Jesus had shared with his disciples during his public life. In support of the Resurrection Peter adds, to the proofs of the empty tomb and the appearances, yet a third: the miracle of Pentecost. This outpouring of the Spirit is a consequence of the Resurrection: those who heard and saw the Spirit manifesting his presence were convinced of the reality of the Paschal fact. An indirect experience, no doubt, for what was seen and heard was a sensible effect of the Resurrection:

> God, then, has raised up this man, Jesus, from the dead; we are all witnesses of it. And now, exalted at God's right

hand, he has claimed from his Father his promise to bestow
the Holy Spirit; and he has poured out that Spirit, as you
can see and hear for yourselves.... Let it be known, then,
beyond all doubt, to all the house of Israel, that God has
made him Master and Christ, this Jesus whom you crucified
(2. 32, 33, 36).

All these details, appearing in the sincerest good faith,
are redolent of the most authentic history, for they are
given by believers who were well acquainted with the Jesus
of whom they spoke. Equally we may note that these details
spring naturally from the Palestinian soil and that period
of the Roman occupation. The person of Pilate is such an
integral part of the story's structure (3. 13; 4. 27; 13. 28)
that the Roman magistrate's name was rightly inscribed
in the cult-formulas, the confessions of faith and the Creed.

With this book of the Acts, we really reach the original
spring which formed the streams from which the synoptic
Gospels were to be born. We hear, without any intermediary,
those men who base their faith on real, precise facts, on
actual words, on a time and places which were well known,
on existing persons: they draw on their own experiences
as well as on the recollections of the holy women and Joseph
of Arimathea, of that "great number of priests" (6. 7) and
those "believers of the party of the Pharisees" (15. 5). We
shall never have a closer view of the story and the mystery
of the God-Man. Not only do the Acts throw light on the
Gospel stories: they even enable us to verify the origin and
the grounds of the Paschal faith itself. "Jesus is risen" is
not a fiction of the evangelists, nor yet of the apostles. It
is the reality which cannot be silenced because it is true.
The fact of Easter sums up in itself alone the whole apostolic
catechesis, so truly is it the central event of the history of
the world and the prophetic sign of the end of the ages.

We must not forget to mention a saying "spoken by the
Lord Jesus himself", which is not to be found anywhere
in the Gospels: "It is more blessed to give than to receive"

(20. 35). St Paul quotes it in his farewell address to the elders of Ephesus gathered at Miletus. It is surely "a sort of ninth Beatitude, escaped from its natural place among those of the Sermon on the Mount" (A. Boudou).

We have not yet spoken of the story of the Ascension, with which the book of the Acts opens. It springs from the Gospel tradition and might equally well have been placed at the end of the third Gospel. It is a precious passage, in more than one respect: not only because it is characteristic of Luke's manner (using an historical element, really verified by the sources, as starting-point for a divine message), but still more for the supplementary information it provides. The majority of the New Testament writings, while affirming the heavenly triumph of Christ after his Resurrection, make no mention of the historical fact of the Ascension. St Luke does indeed say a word about it at the end of his Gospel, but gives the impression that the Resurrection and the Ascension took place on the same day of Easter. In fact, he crowds these events together only because he was reserving it to himself to return to them. The first chapter of the Acts is then the only passage which describes Christ's final parting.

It is indeed an historic memory which Luke means to preserve for us. Everything indicates it; both the sobriety of the narrative, which has nothing in common with the apotheoses of pagan heroes, and the number of details. Detail of time: forty days after the glorious rising from the tomb. Detail of place: on the Mount of Olives. Detail of circumstance: after a meal and a final meeting.

This disappearance into the clouds was not Jesus' entry into glory: the heavenly Exaltation, invisible but real, took place on the very day of the Paschal victory. But it was the visible aspect of that mystery of Christ's penetration for ever into the world of the Spirit, the only palpable experience which men have had of that supernatural reality. This scene in the Acts "represents only the last departure of Christ, required by the sending of the Spirit, and also by the delay ordained by divine Providence before the day of the final restoration (3. 21)" (Fr Benoît).

THE LETTERS OF ST PAUL

About ten years younger than Jesus, Paul of Tarsus, a child of the Diaspora, never lived in the Master's company, never even saw him in "the days of his flesh". Yet who was better informed than he? Who, as he did, had to make a yet deeper study of the story of the Nazarene? While he was still a rabid Pharisee, he heard what was said about Jesus the crucified by the common people and above all by their masters; in the synagogues of Jerusalem he had disputed bitterly with Christ's disciples. Was he not present at that impassioned debate which resulted in the trial and stoning of Stephen (Acts 7. 58)?

Miraculously halted on the Damascus road, he listened in that town to the teaching of Ananias; he lived with the first Christians of Antioch and Jerusalem; he was associated with Barnabas, Silas and Philip the deacon. Anxious to compare his Gospel with that of the official witnesses, he went up to Jerusalem to visit Peter, with whom he stayed two weeks (Gal. 1. 18). On that same occasion he made contact with James the Lord's "brother". Among his companions in the apostolate we find Mark and Luke (Col. 4. 10 and 14), both of whom are named by tradition as biographers of Jesus. Decidedly, "no man was ever better placed to know, fundamentally and in detail, the words and deeds of the Saviour" (F. Prat).

His historical testimony is all the more valuable in that he never experienced, like the Master's close companions, either the temptations or the disappointments; he knew neither the luminous joy of Easter nor the flames of Pentecost, nor the intoxication which accompanied the success of the first preaching. At that period, on the contrary, he so far shared the prejudices of the doctors of Israel as to become a willing persecutor (Gal. 1. 13–14).

Finally, his letters, written as circumstances dictated, appeared at intervals between 50 and 65, and so preceded, at least as regards the most important of them, the publication of the Gospels. We must not expect in them what they did not profess to give, a detailed life of Jesus. That was part of the Christian catechesis, which St Paul had taught before everything else to his correspondents. His letters aim at deepening the teaching they had received, at answering questions put to him by the Churches in the pagan world, at correcting abuses, refuting objections and criticisms, giving news. It is not surprising that he makes only some allusions to the story of Jesus.

But these allusions are precious. They show how thoroughly Paul knew this story. Less than twenty-five years after the date universally assigned to the violent death of Christ under Pontius Pilate, Paul's letters take for their fundamental theme Jesus of Nazareth, his life and his death. Renan writes: "We could make a short life of Jesus from the epistles to the Romans, the Corinthians and the Galatians, and from the epistles to the Hebrews, which is not by St Paul but is very ancient".[1] Let us look at these allusions to the deeds and teachings of Jesus, precious fragments for a Life of Christ, for they tell us the repercussions of those words and deeds on the minds and lives of those first pagan converts, as on the person of the apostle.

The repercussions of Jesus' deeds

The Jesus of Paul is a very live personality, not at all a "metaphysical being". He is someone incontestable, beyond dispute, a being of flesh and blood. His life was lived on earth like ours, only with more suffering.

Jesus is really "a man" (Rom. 5. 12), who "took birth from a woman" (Gal. 4. 4). "Theirs [the patriarchs'] is the human stock from which Christ came" (Rom. 9. 5), "from the line of David" (Rom. 1. 3).

[1] *Histoire du peuple d'Israël* (Paris, 1894), v, p. 416, n. 1.

He had "brothers" or, more accurately, "cousins": Paul had known them, especially the one called James (Gal. 1. 19).

He gathered round him a little community of believers, and from them he chose "twelve" to be his apostles; Cephas, or Peter, and John were well known to Paul (1 Cor. 9. 5; 15. 5–7).

He performed many miracles, for he was "the power of God" (1 Cor. 22–5).

His moral qualities made a strong impression on Paul, who insistently notes his gentleness and courtesy (2 Cor. 10. 1), his fondness for the poor and his effective practice of poverty, with that remarkable phrase which reveals the apostle's astonishment: "You do not need to be reminded how gracious our Lord Jesus Christ was; how he impoverished himself for your sakes, when he was so rich, so that you might become rich through his poverty" (2 Cor. 8. 9); his humility as of a slave and his heroic obedience: it is Paul's hymn to the self-abasements of Christ (Phil. 2. 6–11).

He instituted the Eucharist "on the night when he was being betrayed"; it is to Paul that we owe the earliest account of the Supper, with the details of our Lord's words and actions (1 Cor. 11. 23–5), and that scarcely twenty-five years after that marvellous night!

He was handed over to death (Rom. 4. 25).

He "bore witness to that great claim before Pontius Pilate" (1 Tim. 6. 13). "Christ has been sacrificed for us, our paschal victim" (1 Cor. 5. 7); the Greek word emphasizes that this death is a sacrifice, and the historic past tense refers to a real event. Paul makes much of the blood of Christ as the cause of our redemption (1 Cor. 10. 16; 11. 25 and 27; Rom. 3. 25; 5. 9) and of our incorporation into him (Col. 1. 14 and 20; Eph. 2. 13).

He was crucified (Rom. 6. 5–6). Paul is *par excellence* the preacher of the cross: "What we preach is Christ crucified" (1 Cor. 1. 23); "he lowered his own dignity, accepted an obedience which brought him to death, death on a cross"

(Phil. 2. 8); "God forbid that I should make a display of anything, except the cross of our Lord Jesus Christ" (Gal. 6. 14).

He died (Rom. 5. 6–11; 8. 34; 14. 9). This death of Jesus is to Paul no mere academic truth. He sees in it an ardent love, searching him out: "the Son of God, who loved me and gave himself for me" (Gal. 2. 20); "Order your lives in charity, upon the model of that charity which Christ shewed to us, when he gave himself up on our behalf" (Eph. 5. 2). To see men rejecting the cross of Christ brings tears to his eyes (Phil. 3. 18). And how clearly we can feel the very personal affection in a phrase like this: do not give scandal to the weak conscience, you will risk the loss of his soul, of "thy brother, for whom Christ died" (1 Cor. 8. 11). "Here is a soul for whom Christ died; it is not for thee to bring it to perdition" (Rom. 14. 15).

He was entombed—*etaphé*—(1 Cor. 15. 14): this insistence on the detail in a phrase which has every appearance of being a confession of faith emphasizes that Paul is thinking of a definite tomb—*taphos*—one well known.

He was raised up again: the whole Pauline gospel is expressed in that. Is there a page which is not lit up with the glory of Easter? The Resurrection is Christ's glorification and the cause of our salvation. And above all, let no one dare to speak to Paul of a sort of glorified survival or some vaporous abstraction! For Christ, as for the best of men, it is truly a physical resurrection which is involved, a return to the life of flesh and bones. Paul insists on it. He shows the tragic consequences of any error on this capital point: a Christianity without a dead man raised to life is but wind. In his very first letter Paul notes that it is indeed this person Jesus whom God "raised from the dead" (1 Thess. 1. 10), the same Jesus who, by an action in history, had saved the faithful from the wrath to come.

"He was seen by Cephas, then by the eleven apostles, and afterwards by more than five hundred brethren at once,

most of whom are alive at this day, though some have gone
to their rest. Then he was seen by James, then by all the
apostles; and last of all, I too saw him, like the last child,
that comes to birth unexpectedly" (1 Cor. 15. 5–8). Paul
gives us a list of official testimonies of responsible men who
had yielded only to the plain evidence of the facts.

He is glorified "at the right hand of God" (Rom. 8. 34).

This life of Christ is not something invented by Paul: it
is what was told him by the apostles and first disciples. Paul
is not its original source: he merely hands it on. "The chief
message I handed on to you, as it was handed on to me..."
(1 Cor. 15. 3; 11. 23), that is, the message of tradition. His
agreement with the Twelve is complete and extends not
only to the main facts of the life of Christ but to their
theological interpretation.

To this *man* (1 Tim. 2. 5; Rom. 5. 15), this God-Man,
whose ardent tenderness and incredible kindness he had experienced, Paul devoted a violent love; we see him, with
his fiery character, losing his heart to Jesus with an impetuous
love, as we see him wax indignant against Peter (Gal. 3. 11),
or angry with Barnabas, with a lively disagreement (Acts
15. 39). He loves Jesus with all the obstinacy of his soul,
so much so that whatever is not Christ sickens him: it is
just "refuse" (Phil. 3. 8). He serves Christ against all comers.
He never stops thinking of him, speaking of him, and the
name of Jesus follows him like an obsession. There is more
than a preference, more than a haunting, there is a presence.
He is a man possessed by Christ. Jesus is more than a man
who was dead and is now alive again; he is a man who
causes all other men to live.

Was Paul a dreamer or a poet? His view of faith makes
him, most certainly, a witness to history. Faith is not, for
him, a certain pious or mystical manner of interpreting the
world and the events which occur in it, or a concept of
life ruled only by the heart's intuition, or even a free translation of so-called religious experiences. There is one word

which describes faith for St Paul, a word which constantly
recurs in his writings; it is an *obedience*, a homage (Rom.
1. 5; 16. 26). As such, it presupposes a formal commandment,
expressed by a superior, the Christ, or by his delegates, the
apostles. It does not spring from the heart: it comes from
hearing the word: "See how faith comes from hearing, and
hearing through Christ's word" (Rom. 10. 17).

The repercussions of Jesus' words

Reading St Paul's letters, we hear the echo of Jesus' words
in the first communities of the Christian world. Here too,
we have the Gospel before the Gospels. By collecting all
the admonitions of the letters, one could reconstruct, bit
by bit, the moral teaching of the synoptics.

The number of agreements between St Paul and the
synoptics has been calculated, and the following figures are
those given by Resch: 1 Thess., 63; 2 Thess., 25; 1 Cor.,
214; 2 Cor., 99; Gal., 88; Rom., 270; Col., 81; Eph., 127;
Philem., 10; Phil., 58. As M. Goguel wrote: "Paul had the
incomparable merit of understanding Jesus' thought and reproducing it without altering it in a single point."

The two Letters to the Thessalonians are a still very vivid
echo of the repercussions of Jesus' words in the disciples'
minds, and of the element of Jewish eschatology in his
preaching. Paul uses the same words, the same images, the
same biblical expressions which we find on the lips of Jesus
in St Matthew's Gospel. There are the same counsels to be
vigilant (1 Thess. 5. 4–11) which are found in the synoptic
parables on vigilance. There is again the same uncertainty
about "the times and the seasons", the same idea of the
Jews filling up the measure of their sins, by their resistance
to the preaching of the Gospel (1 Thess. 2. 16 and Matt.
23. 13).

With the two Letters to the Corinthians, we can feel the
full effect of the Master's moral teaching on the daily life
of the converts. On the model of Jesus, Paul warns them

against the wisdom of men, which has nothing to do with the wisdom of God (1 Cor. 18 f. and Mark 8. 33) and against the Jews' childish craze for spectacular miracles (1 Cor. 1. 22 and Matt. 12. 28 f.). He recalls the profound idea of marriage stated in Genesis (1 Cor. 6. 16; 11. 11 and Matt. 19. 5), and in this domain of conjugal morality he is well able to distinguish commands guaranteed by a saying of Jesus from those which have only the authority of his, Paul's, word (1 Cor. 7. 10–12). He insists on the seriousness of scandals (1 Cor. 8. 11–13 and Matt. 5. 29). As for the primacy of charity, the whole of Paul's correspondence orchestrates the "new commandment" of Christ. How could anyone read the "Ode to Agape" (1 Cor. 13) and not be the better for it?

The whole morality of the Letter to the Romans has a distinctly Gospel ring about it, even in its terms. We must not be ashamed of Christ (Rom. 1. 16 and Mark 8. 38); we must not judge others (Rom. 12. 19 and Matt. 7. 1); we must not be like the Pharisees, blind leaders of the blind (Rom. 2. 19 and Matt. 15. 14); "Bless those who curse you" (Rom. 12. 14 and Luke 6. 28). "Do not repay injury with injury" (Rom. 12. 17 and Matt. 5. 39). "It is only when a man believes a thing to be unclean that it becomes unclean for him" (Rom. 14. 14 and Matt. 15. 11).

The Epistle to the Galatians proclaims from end to end the charter of spiritual freedom bestowed by Christ, and the need to crucify the flesh. The Epistle to the Philippians which, more than any other, brings Christ close to us, is scattered with the Master's sayings: "Shine out, beacons to the world" (Phil. 2. 15 and Matt. 5. 14–16); gain and loss for Christ (Phil. 3. 7–8 and Mark 8. 36); we are not to be anxious about worldly things (Phil. 4. 6 and Matt. 6. 25).

It is the same with the Epistles to the Colossians and the Ephesians: the penitent sinner passes from death to life (Eph. 2. 5 and Luke 15. 14, 32); we must pardon as God pardons (Eph. 4. 32 and Matt. 6. 14); we must not trust in the traditions of men (Col. 2. 22 and Matt. 15. 9). And always, earnestly affirmed, the importance of charity among the community (Col. 3. 12–17).

Right down to his last notes to his immediate fellow-workers, Timothy and Titus, we find this care on Paul's part to echo the words of Christ. Jesus has come to save that which was lost (1 Tim. 1. 18 and Luke 15. 2); the apostle has a right to his pay (1 Tim. 5. 18 and Luke 10. 7); accusations must only be accepted when supported by two or three witnesses (1 Tim. 5. 19 and Matt. 18. 16); we must bear witness as Christ did before Pilate (1 Tim. 6. 13 and Matt. 27. 11), for Christ denies the man who denies him (2 Tim. 2. 12 and Matt. 10. 33); we must lay up treasure in heaven (1 Tim. 6. 19 and Matt. 6. 20); reject the hypocrisy of the Pharisees at all times (2 Tim. 3. 5–6 and Matt. 7. 15, 21); "to the pure all things are pure" (Tit. 1. 15 and Matt. 15. 11).

It is plain to see: this is no mythical or purely heavenly being whom Paul proposes as our pattern, but a Jesus of real flesh and blood. When he says to his beloved Corinthians: "Follow my example, as I follow Christ's!" (1 Cor. 4. 16; 11. 1), it is not our Lord's heavenly life that he is indicating as the rule of conduct, in the trials of every day. The last counsel he sends to Timothy, a few weeks before his martyrdom on the road to Ostia, is simply this: "Fix thy mind on Jesus Christ, sprung from the race of David, who has risen from the dead" (2 Tim. 2. 8).

The Epistle to the Hebrews

Our reason for indicating the Epistle to the Hebrews as a source for the story of Christ is that perhaps, or even certainly, no other New Testament document so realistically expresses the profoundly human character of Jesus.

The author's purpose is to prove that Jesus is the one High Priest, whose priesthood, begun on earth, is fully exercized in the sanctuary of heaven. In order to lead men to perfection, the High Priest must himself have gone through the different stages of a human life. He must have been fully man: "The purpose for which any high priest is chosen *from among men*" (5. 1)... This indicates how completely Jesus was man.

But then we have this declaration, which would be the most bewildering of all, if we did not know how sincerely the Son of Man willed to live his earthly life: "It is not as if our high priest were incapable of feeling for us in our humiliations: he has been through every trial, fashioned as we are, only sinless" (4. 15). Such an assertion, made with such emphasis, at first sight surprises, almost shocks us!

It is clear that the author does not allude merely to the Messianic temptation recorded by the synoptics at the beginning of his public ministry, nor even to those frequent trials which Christ, at grips with his bitter and bigoted enemies, had to face (Mark 8. 33; 12. 15). Prof. Cullmann, who has carefully analysed this passage, writes: "It truly refers to that general temptation, due to our human weakness, to which we are all exposed from the mere fact that we are men. This expression 'as we are' is not merely formal: it has a profound meaning."[2]

No; neither in the synoptics nor in St John, nor even in St Paul, do we meet with a remark of such realism. A simple note, but with what echoes! A very brief flash, but what light it throws on the inner life of that man, Jesus of Nazareth! No doubt we shall never know the precise nature of those inner trials, and it would be a kind of sacrilege to try to pierce the secret, but how it makes Jesus one of us! He was tempted in all things like ourselves; only, he never yielded.

This inclusion of Jesus in the very stuff of our humanity is again indicated in another passage of this epistle. Many authors think it refers to the agony in Gethsemani: "Christ, during his earthly life, offered prayer and entreaty to the God who could save him from death, not without a piercing

[2] O. Cullmann, *Christologie du Nouveau Testament*, Neuchâtel, 1955, p. 84.

cry, not without tears; yet with such piety as won him a hearing" (5. 7). The detail is absolutely original. We learn that in that fearful nocturnal struggle Christ emerged victorious from the most violent of temptations only after he had long prayed, cried out, wept.

This full humanity of Jesus is again defined by another touch: "Son of God though he was, he learned obedience in the school of suffering" (5. 8). Jesus *learned* obedience! There was in him a certain development, a sort of moral progress, which was to reach its summit in the bloody obedience of Calvary. St Luke tells how he "advanced in wisdom with the years and in favour both with God and with men" (Luke 2. 52), and St Paul speaks of a progress towards even deeper humiliation: accepting "an obedience which brought him to death, death on a cross" (Phil. 2. 8).

Plainly, our author is not afraid to deduce all the consequences of the incarnation of Jesus. Jesus was fully man: just as he is fully God. He is equally bold in affirming Christ's divinity, since the Son is invoked as the creator of heaven and earth (1. 10).

As a final historical detail, we learn that Jesus "suffered beyond the city gate" (13. 12), that is, outside the ramparts of Jerusalem.

The Catholic Epistles

These do not tell us anything very new. To Jude, Jesus Christ is "Master and Lord" (4); he speaks through the apostles (17) and it is he who will have mercy on Christians so as to give them eternal life (21). James makes only two very short allusions to Jesus (1. 1; 2. 1). The first Epistle of Peter tells us that Jesus, between his death and resurrection, "went and preached to the spirits who lay in prison" (3. 19), and that he was spotless in his innocence (1. 19; 2. 22). From the second Epistle we glean that precious allusion to the scene of the Transfiguration, when "a voice came to him out of the splendour which dazzles human eyes; This, it

said, is my beloved Son, in whom I am well pleased." And
St Peter adds: "We, his companions on the holy mountain,
heard the voice coming from heaven" (1. 17–18).

From the three Epistles of St John we shall recall only
the beginning of the first: with as much gravity as emotion
the aged apostle declares that the Word of Life, that eternal
Being, is indeed the same as the historical Jesus, and in
the name of all the eye-witnesses, his own name above all,
John describes that direct, personal experience of the fact
he attests: "Our message concerns that Word, who is life;
what he was from the first, what we have heard about him,
what our own eyes have seen of him; what it was that met
our gaze, and the touch of our hands. Yes, life dawned;
and it is as eye-witnesses that we give you news of that life"
(1. 1–2).

CHAPTER VI

ANCIENT CHRISTIAN TEXTS ON THE ORIGIN OF THE GOSPELS

by François Amiot, P.S.S.

From the closing years of the first century and throughout the second, the Gospels were quoted and used by the Apostolic Fathers; St Clement of Rome (about 95), St Ignatius of Antioch (107–17), St Polycarp of Smyrna (108–18), the so-called *Epistle of Barnabas* (100–30), the *Shepherd* of Hermas (115–30) and the *Didache* or *Teaching of the Apostles* (130–40). These documents do not name the authors of the Gospels, but they quote them, St John as well as the synoptics, in a manner sufficiently characteristic to enable us to affirm that they were already well known. This conclusion is reinforced by the testimony of the papyri recently discovered in Egypt (the Egerton and John Rylands), which date from the first half of the second century and contain fragments of the four Gospels; they supply proof that all, and especially St John's, were used about thirty years after the latter's composition and a long way from Ephesus, its place of origin. It was therefore accorded from the beginning the same authority as the synoptics; a fact of obvious importance.

In the middle of the second century, a period of synthesis when the Church was becoming more clearly conscious of the treasure she possessed, she insisted on the fact that the

Gospels were the "Memoirs of the apostles and their disciples"; they were thus described, about 160–7, by the philosopher and martyr St Justin (*Apologia* I, 66, 3; *Dialogue with Trypho the Jew*, 103, 8); he quotes a passage of St Mark (3. 17) under the name of "Memoirs of St Peter".

He thus agrees with the rather earlier and more precise testimony of Papias, bishop of Hierapolis in Phrygia, which has been preserved by St Irenaeus (*Adversus haereses*, III, 33, 4) and by Eusebius (*Hist. eccles.*, 3, 39). Papias claims to be reproducing the sayings of several apostles, Peter, Philip, Thomas, James, John and Matthew, which had come down to him through disciples belonging to the next generation, Aristion and John the Presbyter. The identification of this John with the evangelist is a disputed point; but even if he is a different person, the tradition which attributes the fourth Gospel to the apostle is still valid, for it does not depend on Papias, as we shall see. This is what Papias says on the subject of the first two Gospels:

> The Presbyter said this also: Mark, having become the interpreter of Peter, wrote down accurately everything that he remembered, without however recording in order what was either said or done by Christ. For neither did he hear the Lord, nor did he follow him; but afterwards, as I said, [attended] Peter, who adapted his instructions to the needs [of his hearers] but had no design of giving a connected account of the Lord's oracles. So then Mark made no mistake, while he thus wrote down some things as he remembered them; for he made it his one care not to omit anything that he heard, or to set down any false statement therein.
>
> Such then is the account given by Papias concerning Mark. But concerning Matthew, the following statement is made [by him]: "So then Matthew composed the oracles in the Hebrew language, and each one interpreted them as he could."
>
> (*Trans.* H. M. Gwatkin, *Selections from Early Christian Writers* (London, 1905), p. 82 f.)

What he describes as Mark's lack of order is actually in general agreement with the chronological order; Papias here contrasts it with the beautiful didactic order of St Matthew, whom he evidently prefers, emphasizing that he devotes more space to Christ's sayings.

By about 175–200, the Gospels were known all round the Mediterranean basin. This is proved by Tatian's *Diatessaron,* the first "harmony" of the four Gospels, by several Syriac versions and by an ancient Latin version, the Italic, the existence of which seems to be attested in the Acts of the Scillitan Martyrs, in Numidia.

After this period the testimonies are very explicit. The *Muratorian Canon,* a list of books of the New Testament, which was discovered in 1750 by the scholar Muratori, in the Ambrosian Library at Milan, and may be dated about 200, quotes the third Gospel as being that of St Luke (it had previously mentioned Matthew and Mark, but the beginning of the text is mutilated).

> The third book of the Gospel, that according to Luke, was compiled in his own name in order by Luke the physician, when after Christ's ascension Paul had taken him to be with him like a student of law. Yet neither did *he* see the Lord in the flesh[1]; and he too, as he was able to ascertain [events], began his story from the birth of John.

Then on the subject of St John it says:

> The fourth of the gospels [was written by] John, one of the disciples. When exhorted by his fellow-disciples and bishops, he said, Fast with me this day for three days; and what may be revealed to any of us, let us relate it to one another. The same night it was revealed to Andrew, one of the apostles, that John was to write all things in his own name, and they were all to certify. And therefore, though various elements are taught in the several books of the Gospels, yet it makes no difference to the faith of believers, since by one guiding Spirit all things are declared in all of them concerning the Nativity, the Passion, the Resurrection, the conversation with

[1] The lost part of the text therefore indicated that Mark had not been an eye-witness of Christ's life.

his disciples and his two comings, the first in lowliness and contempt, which has come to pass, the second glorious with royal power, which is to come. What marvel therefore if John so firmly sets forth each statement in his Epistle too, saying of himself, What things we have seen with our eyes and heard with our ears and our hands have handled, these things we have written to you?[2] For so he declares himself not an eye-witness and a hearer only, but a writer of all the marvels of the Lord in order. (*Trans.* H. M. Gwatkin, *ibid.*, pp. 83–5.)

In spite of certain legendary details, this text significantly insists on the authority attributed to the fourth Gospel, equally with the first three. It next mentions the Acts and the Epistles.

St Irenaeus, a disciple of St Polycarp of Smyrna (himself a disciple of St John the apostle), was bishop of Lyons, in regular communication with the Church in Rome, and his testimony (about 181–9) is therefore very important. It echoes a well-established tradition which leaves no room for doubt.

Matthew published a written gospel among the Hebrews in their own language, while Peter and Paul were preaching and founding the Church in Rome. After their decease [or, *departure?*] Mark, the disciple and interpreter of Peter—he also transmitted to us in writing those things which Peter had preached; and Luke, the attendant of Paul, recorded in a book the Gospel which Paul had declared. Afterwards John, the disciple of the Lord, who also reclined on his bosom— he too published the Gospel, while staying at Ephesus in Asia. (*Adversus haereses*, III, 1, 1; quoted by Eusebius, *Hist. eccles.*, V, 8. *Trans.* Gwatkin, *ibid.*, p. 89.)

As there are four quarters in the world, and four principal winds, and as the Church is spread throughout all the world, having the Gospel as its pillar and support, it is natural that there should be four pillars, everywhere breathing out immortality and life to men. From this it is clear that the Word ... has given us the tetramorphic Gospel, governed by one only Spirit.... This being the case, they are foolish, senseless

[2] I John 1. 1.

and even presumptuous, who destroy the form of the Gospel, and deceitfully introduce either more or less persons than have been told us. (*Adversus haereses*, III, 11, 8–9.)

In Egypt, about 200, Clement of Alexandria expressed himself thus:

> As regards the order of the gospels, Clement confirmed the tradition of the ancient elders, which is as follows. He says that the gospels containing the genealogies were written before the others. Mark's was undertaken in the following way: Peter was publicly preaching the word of God in Rome and expounding the Gospel under the inspiration of the Spirit; those who had attended his preaching—and they were many— urged Mark, who had long accompanied Peter and remembered his sayings, to commit them to writing. He did so and gave the Gospel to those who had asked for it. Peter heard of this and did nothing by his advice either to stop it or to encourage it. John, however, the last of all, seeing that the gospels set forth only the material side of the story, entreated by his disciples and divinely inspired by the Spirit, wrote *a spiritual gospel*. (*Hypotyposes*, quoted by Eusebius, *Hist. eccles.*, VI, 14, 5 f.)

The statement about the priority of the Gospels with the genealogies, contradicted by all the other witnesses, is certainly mistaken. Elsewhere (a passage quoted in *Eusebius* II, 15) Clement echoes a tradition that Peter was pleased at the publication of the second Gospel. Finally, in his *Stromata*, I, 21, he mentions St Luke and St Matthew and quotes the beginnings of their Gospels.

Soon after 244, again in Egypt, Origen, the illustrious exegete and theologian, adds this precise testimony:

> I have learned, as part of the tradition about the four gospels, which alone are undisputed in the Church of God under heaven, that the first book is that of Matthew, at first a publican, then an apostle of Jesus Christ: it was addressed to those who had passed from Judaism to the new law, and was composed in the Hebrew tongue. The second is that of Mark, who

wrote it according to the instructions of Peter, who attests in his Catholic epistle that Mark was his son, speaking of him in these terms: "the Church which is in Babylon salutes you, and Mark my son".[3] The third is Luke's, the gospel praised by Paul and composed for the Gentiles. After all these comes that of John. (*Commentary on St Matthew*, quoted by Eusebius, *Hist. eccles.*, VI, 25.)

In Africa a little earlier, about 207, the apologist Tertullian states that the Gospels are the work of two apostles, John and Matthew, and two of their disciples, Luke and Mark (*Adversus Marcionem*, IV, 2). St Cyprian, bishop of Carthage, martyred in 258, quotes the Gospels so often— although, no doubt accidentally, he does not name the authors —that with the aid of his works one could reconstruct the Latin version he used.

Finally, in the fourth century, the historian Eusebius of Caesarea, who died in 340 (*Hist. eccles.*, III, 4 and 2), and later St Jerome, the translator of our Latin Vulgate, who died in 420 (*De Viris Illustribus*, Migne, *P.L.*, XXIII, 613, 3 f.; *Commentary on St Matthew*, Prologues, *ibid.*, XXVI, 18–19), recapitulate tradition and record some supplementary tradition about the composition of Matthew in Aramaic, Mark's dependence on St Peter and Luke's on St Paul, and St John's purpose of supplementing the synoptics.

To sum up—the Gospels are always and everywhere accepted; there is no hesitation about their names (the apocryphal gospels are formally excluded) nor on the order of their appearance (with the negligible exception of Clement of Alexandria). Their origin is stated to be apostolic (Matthew and John) or at least equivalent (Mark and Luke), and this point is evidently held to be essential.

[3] I Peter, 5. 13.

SELECT BIBLIOGRAPHY

In this series: DANIEL-ROPS: *What is the Bible?*; STEINMANN, J.: *Biblical Criticism.*

ADAM, Karl: *Christ our Brother*, London, Sheed and Ward, and New York, Macmillan, 1931; *The Son of God*, London, Sheed and Ward, 1940; *The Christ of Faith*, London, Burns and Oates, 1961, and New York, Pantheon, 1957.

ALECH, Matthew: *The Scrolls and Christian Origins*, London and New York, Nelson, 1961.

BUTLER, B. C.: *The Originality of St Matthew*, Cambridge and New York, Cambridge Univ. Press, 1957.

CERFAUX, L.: *Christ in the Theology of St Paul*, London and New York, Nelson, 1959; *The Four Gospels*, London, Darton, Longman and Todd, 1960.

CHAPMAN, John, O.S.B.: *The Four Gospels*, London and New York, Sheed and Ward, 1944.

CHARLIER, C.: *The Christian Approach to the Bible*, London, Sands, 1957.

CROSS, F. M.: *The Ancient Library of Qumran*, London, Gerald Duckworth, 1958.

DANIEL-ROPS: *Jesus in his Time*, London, Burns and Oates, 1955, and New York, Dutton, 1954.

DELL-ISOLA, F.: *The God-Man Jesus*, Milwaukee, Bruce, 1960.

DUPONT-SOMMER, A.: *The Jewish Sect of Qumran and the Essenes*, London, Secker and Warburg, 1954, and New York, Macmillan, 1955.

GASTER, T. H.: *The Scriptures of the Dead Sea Sect* (translation of text), London, Secker and Warburg, 1957, and New York, Doubleday, 1956.

GOODIER, A.: *The Public Life of Our Lord Jesus Christ*, London, Burns and Oates, and New York, Kenedy, 1941; *The Passion and Death of Our Lord Jesus Christ*, London, Burns and Oates, and New York, Kenedy, 1958.

GRANDMAISON, L. de: *Jesus Christ, His Person, His Life, His Credentials*, London, Sheed and Ward, 1935.

GRAYSTONE, G.: *The Dead Sea Scrolls and the Originality of Christ*, London and New York, Sheed and Ward, 1956.

GUARDINI, R.: *The Lord*, London, Sheed and Ward, 1956, and Chicago, Regnery, 1954.

HARRISON, R. K.: *The Dead Sea Scrolls*, London, English Universities Press, 1961.

JOHNSTON, L.: *Witnesses to God*, London, Sheed and Ward, 1960.

JONES, Alex: *God's Living Word*, London, Geoffrey Chapman, 1961.

KENYON, Sir F.: *Our Bible and the Ancient Manuscripts*, London, Eyre and Spottiswoode, 1958.

LAGRANGE, M. J.: *The Gospel of Jesus Christ* (two volumes), London, Burns and Oates, 1947, and Westminster, Md, Newman Press, 1943.

LEBRETON, J.: *The Life and Teaching of Jesus Christ* (revised edn, two volumes), London, Burns and Oates, and New York, Macmillan, 1935; *The Spiritual Teaching of the New Testament*, London, Burns and Oates, 1960.

MAURIAC, F.: *The Life of Christ*, London, Peter Davies, 1949, and New York, McKay, 1951.

MONRO, Margaret: *Enjoying the New Testament*, London and New York, Longmans, 1945.

PLOEG, J. v.d.: *The Excavations at Qumran*, London, Longmans, 1958.

PRAT, F.: *Jesus Christ* (two volumes), Milwaukee, Bruce, 1950.

RICCIOTTI, G.: *The Life of Christ*, Cork, Mercier Press, 1959, and Milwaukee, Bruce, 1947.

ROWLEY, H. H.: *The Dead Sea Scrolls and their Significance*, London, Independent Press, and New York, Allenson, 1955; *The Dead Sea Scrolls and the New Testament*, London, S.P.C.K., 1957.

SCHUBERT, K.: *The Dead Sea Community*, London, A. and C. Black, 1959.

SHEEN, F.: *The Life of Christ*, London, Peter Davies, 1958.

SOWTER, A.: *The Text and Canon of the New Testament* (second edn, revised Wilkinson), London, Gerald Duckworth, 1954.

SUTCLIFFE, E. F.: *The Monks of Qumran*, London, Burns and Oates, and Westminster, Md, Newman Press, 1960.

TAYLOR, Vincent: *The Text of the New Testament*, London, Macmillan, 1961.

THOMPSON, J. M.: *The Synoptic Gospels arranged in Parallel Columns*, London and New York, Oxford Univ. Press, 1910.

VONIER, A.: *The Personality of Christ* (volume II in Collected Works), London, Burns and Oates, and Westminster, Md, Newman Press, 1952.

WIKENHAUSER, A.: *New Testament Introduction*, London, Nelson, 1959.